# HOW TO READ LITERATURE

# HOW TO READ
# LITERATURE
## TERRY EAGLETON

YALE UNIVERSITY PRESS
NEW HAVEN AND LONDON

For information about this and other Yale University Press publications, please contact:

U.S. Office: sales.press@yale.edu    www.yalebooks.com
Europe Office: sales @yaleup.co.uk    www.yalebooks.co.uk

Set in Arno Pro by IDSUK (DataConnection) Ltd
Printed in the United States of America

Library of Congress Cataloging-in-Publication Data

Eagleton, Terry, 1943-
    How to read literature / Terry Eagleton.
        pages cm
    ISBN 978-0-300-19096-0 (cl : alk. paper)
1. Literature—Philosophy. 2. Authors and readers. 3. Reader-response criticism.
4. Literature—Explication. I. Title.
    PN49.E25 2013
    801—dc23
                                                                2013001802

A catalogue record for this book is available from the British Library.

10 9 8 7 6 5 4 3 2 1

For permission to reprint poetry extracts from copyright material the publishers gratefully acknowledge Farrar, Straus and Giroux for lines from Robert Lowell's 'The Quaker Graveyard in Nantucket'; and Faber and Faber Ltd, and Farrar, Straus and Giroux for lines from Philip Larkin's 'The Trees' and 'Whitsun Weddings'.

In memory of
Adrian and Angela Cunningham

# Contents

# Preface

Like clog dancing, the art of analysing works of literature is almost dead on its feet. A whole tradition of what Nietzsche called 'slow reading' is in danger of sinking without trace. By paying close attention to literary form and technique, this book tries to play a modest part in riding to its rescue. It is mainly intended as a guide for beginners, but I hope it will also prove useful to those already engaged in literary studies, or those who simply enjoy reading poems, plays and novels in their spare time. I try to shed some light on such questions as narrative, plot, character, literary language, the nature of fiction, problems of critical interpretation, the role of the reader and the question of value judgements. The book also puts forward some ideas about individual authors, as well as about such literary currents as classicism, romanticism, modernism and realism, for those who might feel in need of them.

I am, I suppose, best known as a literary theorist and political critic, and some readers might wonder what has become of these interests in this book. The answer is that one cannot raise political or theoretical questions about literary texts without a degree of sensitivity to their language. My concern here is to provide readers and students with some of the basic tools of the critical trade, without which they are unlikely to be able to move on to other matters. I hope to show in the process that critical analysis can be fun, and in doing so help to demolish the myth that analysis is the enemy of enjoyment.

TE

# CHAPTER 1

# Openings

Imagine that you are listening to a group of students around a seminar table discussing Emily Brontë's novel *Wuthering Heights*. The conversation might go something like this:

*Student A:* I can't see what's so great about Catherine's relationship with Heathcliff. They're just a couple of squabbling brats.

*Student B:* Well, it's not really a *relationship* at all, is it? It's more like a mystical unity of selves. You can't talk about it in everyday language.

*Student C:* Why not? Heathcliff's not a mystic, he's a brute. The guy's not some kind of Byronic hero; he's vicious.

*Student B:* OK, so who made him like that? The people at the Heights, of course. He was fine when he was a child. They think he's not good enough to marry Catherine so he turns into a monster. At least he's not a wimp like Edgar Linton.

*Student A:* Sure, Linton's a bit spineless, but he treats Catherine a lot better than Heathcliff does.

What is wrong with this discussion? Some of the points made are fairly perceptive. Everybody seems to have read their way beyond page 5. Nobody seems to think that Heathcliff is a small town in Kansas. The problem is that if someone who had never heard of *Wuthering Heights* were to listen in on this discussion, they would find nothing to suggest that it was about a *novel*. Perhaps a listener might assume that the students were gossiping about some rather peculiar friends of theirs. Maybe Catherine is a student in the School of Business Studies, Edgar Linton is Dean of Arts and Heathcliff is a psychopathic janitor. Nothing is said about the techniques by which the novel builds up its characters. Nobody raises the question of what attitudes the book itself takes up towards these figures. Are its judgements always consistent, or might they be ambiguous? What about the novel's imagery, symbolism and narrative structure? Do they reinforce what we feel about its characters, or do they undercut it?

Of course, as the debate continued, it might become clearer that the students were arguing about a novel. Some of the time, it is hard to distinguish what literary critics say about poems and novels from talk about real life. There is no great crime in that. These days, however, this can be true for rather too much of the time. The most common mistake students of literature make is to go straight for what the poem or novel says, setting aside the way that it says it. To read like this is to set aside the 'literariness' of the work – the fact that it is a poem or play or novel, rather than an account of the incidence of soil erosion in Nebraska. Literary works are pieces of rhetoric as well as reports. They demand a peculiarly vigilant kind of reading, one which is alert to tone, mood, pace, genre, syntax, grammar, texture, rhythm, narrative structure, punctuation, ambiguity – in fact to everything that comes under the heading of 'form'. It is true that one could always read a report on soil erosion in Nebraska in this 'literary' way. It would simply mean paying close attention to the workings of its language. For some literary theorists, this would be enough to turn it into a work of literature, though probably not one to rival *King Lear*.

Part of what we mean by a 'literary' work is one in which *what* is said is to be taken in terms of *how* it is said. It is the kind of writing in which the content is inseparable from the language in which it is presented. Language is constitutive of the reality or experience, rather than simply a vehicle for it. Take a road sign reading 'Roadworks: Expect Long Delays on the Ramsbottom Bypass for the Next Twenty-Three Years'. Here, the language is simply a vehicle for a thought that could be expressed in a whole variety of ways. An enterprising local authority might even put it in verse. If they were unsure of how long the bypass would be out of action, they might always rhyme 'Close' with 'God knows'. 'Lillies that fester smell far worse than weeds,' by contrast, is a lot harder to paraphrase, at least without ruining the line altogether. And this is one of several things we mean by calling it poetry.

To say that we should look at what is done in a literary work in terms of how it is done is not to claim that the two always slot neatly together. You could, for example, recount the life-history of a field mouse in Miltonic blank verse. Or you could write about your yearning to be free in a strict, straitjacketing kind of metre. In cases like this, the form would be interestingly at odds with the content. In his novel *Animal Farm*, George Orwell casts the complex history of the Bolshevik Revolution into the form of an apparently simple fable about farmyard animals. In such cases, critics might want to talk of a tension between form and content. They might see this discrepancy as part of the meaning of the work.

The students we have just overheard wrangling have conflicting views about *Wuthering Heights*. This raises a whole series of questions, which strictly speaking belong more to literary theory than to literary criticism. What is involved in interpreting a text? Is there a right and a wrong way of doing so? Can we demonstrate that one interpretation is more valid than another? Could there be a true account of a novel that nobody has yet come up with, or that nobody ever will? Could Student A and Student B both be right about Heathcliff, even though their views of him are vigorously opposed?

Perhaps the people around the table have grappled with these questions, but a good many students these days have not. For them, the act of reading is a fairly innocent one. They are not aware of how fraught a matter it is just to say 'Heathcliff'. After all, there is a sense in which Heathcliff does not exist, so it seems strange to talk about him as though he does. It is true that there are theorists of literature who think that literary characters do exist. One of them believes that the starship *Enterprise* really does have a heat shield. Another considers that Sherlock Holmes is a creature of flesh and blood. Yet another argues that Dickens's Mr Pickwick is real, and that his servant Sam Weller can see him, even though we cannot. These people are not clinically insane, simply philosophers.

There is a connection, overlooked in the students' conversation, between their own disputes and the structure of the novel itself. *Wuthering Heights* tells its story in a way that involves a variety of viewpoints. There is no 'voice-over' or single trustworthy narrator to guide the reader's responses. Instead, we have a series of reports, some probably more reliable than others, each stacked inside each other like Chinese boxes. The book interweaves one mini-narrative with another, without telling us what to make of the characters and events it portrays. It is in no hurry to let us know whether Heathcliff is hero or demon, Nelly Dean shrewd or stupid, Catherine Earnshaw tragic heroine or spoilt brat. This makes it difficult for readers to pass definitive judgements on the story, and the difficulty is increased by its garbled chronology.

We may contrast this 'complex seeing', as it has been called, with the novels of Emily's sister Charlotte. Charlotte's *Jane Eyre* is narrated from one viewpoint only, that of the heroine herself, and the reader is meant to assume that what Jane says, goes. No character in the book is allowed to deliver an account of the proceedings that would seriously challenge her own. We, the readers, may suspect that what Jane has to report is not always without a touch of self-interest or the occasional hint of malice. But the novel itself does not seem to recognise this.

In *Wuthering Heights*, by contrast, the partial, biased nature of the characters' accounts is built into the structure of the book. We are alerted to it early on, as we come to realise that Lockwood, the novel's chief narrator, is hardly the brightest man in Europe. There are times when he has only a slender grasp of the Gothic events unfolding around him. Nelly Dean is a prejudiced storyteller who has her knife into Heathcliff, and whose narrative cannot wholly be trusted. How the story is seen from the world of Wuthering Heights is at odds with how it is viewed from the neighbouring Thrushcross Grange. Yet there is something to be said for both of these ways of looking, even when they are at loggerheads with each other. Heathcliff may be both a brutal sadist and an abused outcast. Catherine may be both a petulant child and a grown woman in search of her fulfilment. The novel itself does not invite us to choose. Instead, it allows us to hold these conflicting versions of reality in tension. Which is not to suggest that we are necessarily to tread some sensible middle path between them. Middle paths in tragedy are in notably short supply.

It is important, then, not to confuse fiction with reality, which the students around the table seem in danger of doing. Prospero, the hero of Shakespeare's *The Tempest*, comes forward at the end of the play to warn the audience against making this mistake; but he does so in a way that suggests that confusing art with the real world can diminish its effects on that world:

> *Now my charms are all o'erthrown,*
> *And what strength I have's mine own,*
> *Which is most faint. Now, 'tis true,*
> *I must be here confined by you,*
> *Or sent to Naples. Let me not,*
> *Since I have my dukedom got*
> *And pardoned the deceiver, dwell*
> *In this bare island by your spell,*
> *But release me from my bands*
> *With the help of your good hands.*

What Prospero is doing is asking the audience to applaud. This is one thing he means by 'With the help of your good hands.' By applauding, the spectators in the theatre will acknowledge that what they have been watching is a piece of fiction. If they fail to recognise this, it is as though they and the figures on stage will remain trapped for ever inside the dramatic illusion. The actors will be unable to leave the stage, and the audience will remain frozen in the auditorium. This is why Prospero speaks of the danger of being confined to his magic island 'by your spell', meaning by the audience's reluctance to let go of the fantasy they have been enjoying. Instead, they must use their hands to clap and so release him, as though he is bound fast in their imaginative fiction and unable to move. In doing so, the spectators confess that this is simply a piece of drama; but to make this confession is essential if the drama is to have real effects. Unless they applaud, abandon the theatre and return to the real world, they will be unable to put to use whatever the play has revealed to them. The spell must be broken if the magic is to work. In fact, there was a belief at the time that a magic spell could be broken by noise, which is yet another meaning of Prospero's appeal to the audience to clap.

\* \* \*

Learning how to be a literary critic is, among other things, a matter of learning how to deploy certain techniques. Like a lot of techniques – scuba-diving, for example, or playing the trombone – these are more easily picked up in practice than in theory. All of them involve a closer attention to language than one would usually lavish on a recipe or a laundry list. In this chapter, then, I aim to provide some practical exercises in literary analysis, taking as my texts the first lines or sentences of various well-known literary works.

A word first of all about literary beginnings. Endings in art are absolute, in the sense that once a figure like Prospero vanishes he vanishes for ever. We cannot ask whether he ever really made it back to his dukedom, since he does not survive the play's final line. There is a sense in which literary openings are absolute too. This is clearly not true in every sense. Almost all literary works begin by using words that have been used countless times before, though not necessarily in this particular combination. We can grasp the meaning of these opening sentences only because we come to them with a frame of cultural reference which allows us to do so. We also approach them with some conception of what a literary work is, what is meant by a beginning, and so on. In this sense, no literary opening is ever really absolute. All reading involves a fair amount of stage setting. A lot of things must already be in place simply for a text to be intelligible. One of them is previous works of literature. Every literary work harks back, if only unconsciously, to other works. Yet the opening of a poem or novel also seems to spring out of a kind of silence, since it inaugurates a fictional world that did not exist before. Perhaps it is the closest thing we have to the act of divine Creation, as some Romantic artists believed. The difference is that we are stuck with the Creation, whereas we can always discard our copy of Catherine Cookson.

Let us begin with the opening sentences of one of the most celebrated of twentieth-century novels, E.M. Forster's *A Passage to India*:

> Except for the Marabar Caves – and they are twenty miles off – the city of Chandrapore presents nothing extraordinary. Edged rather than washed by the river Ganges, it trails for a couple of miles along the bank, scarcely distinguishable from the rubbish it deposits so freely. There are no bathing-steps on the river front, as the Ganges happens not to be holy here; indeed there is no river front, and bazaars shut out the wide and shifting panorama of the stream. The streets are mean, the temples ineffective, and though a few fine houses exist they are hidden away in gardens or down alleys whose filth deters all but the invited guest . . .

As with the opening of a lot of novels, there is something of a setpiece feel to this, as the author clears his throat and formally sets the scene. A writer tends to be on his or her best behaviour at the beginning of Chapter 1, eager to impress, keen to catch the fickle reader's eye, and occasionally intent on pulling out all the stops. Even so, he must beware of overdoing it, not least if he is a civilised middle-class Englishman like E.M. Forster who values reticence and indirectness. Perhaps this is one reason why the passage opens with a throwaway qualification ('Except for the Marabar Caves') rather than with a blare of verbal trumpets. It sidles into its subject-matter sideways, rather than confronting it head-on. 'The city of Chandrapore presents nothing extraordinary, except for the Marabar Caves, and they are twenty miles off' would be far too ungraceful. It would spoil the poise of the syntax, which is elegant in an unshowy kind of way. It is deftly managed and manipulated, but with quiet good manners refuses to rub this in one's face. There is no suggestion of 'fine writing', or of what is sometimes called 'purple' (excessively ornate) prose. The author's eye is too closely on the object for any such self-indulgence.

The first two clauses of the novel hold off the subject of the sentence ('the city of Chandrapore') twice over, so that the reader experiences a slight quickening of expectations before finally arriving at this phrase. One's expectations, however, are aroused only to be deflated, since we are told that the city contains nothing remarkable. More exactly, we are told rather oddly that there is nothing remarkable about the city except for the Caves, but that the Caves are not in the city. We are also informed that there are no bathing steps on the river front, but that there is no river front.

The four phrases of the first sentence are almost metrical in their rhythm and balance. In fact, it is possible to read them as trimeters, or lines of verse with three stresses each:

> *Except for the **Marabar Caves***
> *And **they** are **twenty** miles **off***
> *The **city** of **Chandrapore***
> *Presents **nothing** extraordinary*

The same delicate equipoise crops up in the phrase 'Edged rather than washed', which is perhaps a touch too fastidious. This is a writer with a keenly discriminating eye, but also a coolly distancing one. In traditional English style, he refuses to get excited or enthusiastic (the city 'presents nothing extraordinary'). The word 'presents' is significant. It makes Chandrapore sound like a show put on for the sake of a spectator, rather than a place to be lived in. 'Presents nothing extraordinary' to whom? The answer is surely to the tourist. The tone of the passage – disenchanted, slightly supercilious, a touch overbred – is that of a rather snooty guidebook. It sails as close as it dares to suggesting that the city is literally a heap of garbage.

The importance of tone as an indication of attitude is made clear in the novel itself. Mrs Moore, an Englishwoman who has just arrived in colonial India and is unaware of British cultural habits there, tells her imperial-minded son Ronny about her encounter with a young Indian doctor in a temple. Ronny does not initially realise that she is talking about a 'native', and when he does so becomes instantly irritable and suspicious. 'Why hadn't she indicated by the tone of her voice that she was talking about an Indian?' he thinks to himself.

As far as the tone of this passage goes, we may note among other things the triple alliteration of the phrase 'happens not to be holy here', which trots somewhat too glibly off the tongue. It represents a wry poke at Hindu beliefs on the part of a sceptical, sophisticated outsider. The alliteration suggests a 'cleverness', a discreet delight in verbal artifice, which puts a distance between the narrator and the poverty-stricken city. The same is true of the lines 'The streets are mean, the temples ineffective, and though a few fine houses exist . . .' The syntax of this is a little too self-consciously contrived, too obviously intent on a 'literary' effect.

So far, the passage has managed to keep this shabby Indian city at arm's length without sounding too offensively superior, but the word 'ineffective' to describe the temples almost deliberately gives the game away. Though the syntax tucks it unobtrusively away in a sub-clause, it strikes the reader like a mild smack in the face. The term assumes that the temples are there not for the inhabitants to worship in, but for the observer to take pleasure in. They are ineffective in the sense that they do nothing for the artistically-minded tourist. The adjective makes them sound like flat tyres or broken radios. In fact, it does this so calculatedly that one wonders, perhaps a little too charitably, whether it is meant to be ironic. Is this narrator sending up his own high-handed manner?

It is clear enough that the narrator, who is not necessarily to be identified with the historical individual E.M. Forster, has some inside knowledge of India. He has not just stepped off the boat. He knows, for example, that the Ganges is sometimes sacred and sometimes not. Perhaps he is implicitly comparing Chandrapore to other cities in the sub-continent. There is a slightly jaded air about the extract, as though the narrator has seen too much of this country to be easily impressed. Perhaps the paragraph aims to deflate the Romantic view of India as exotic and enigmatic. The title of the book, *A Passage to India*, may breed such expectations in the Western reader, which the novel then mischievously undercuts right from the outset. Maybe these lines are quietly enjoying their effect on the kind of reader who was expecting something a little more mysterious than filth and rubbish.

Speaking of filth, why is it that the dirty alleys leading to the finer houses deter all but the invited guest? Presumably because an invited guest, unlike a casual tourist, has no choice about negotiating them. There is the ghost of a joke here: it is the most privileged people, those fortunate enough to be invited to the fine houses, who are forced to pick a path through the mud. To claim that these guests are not deterred by the garbage makes them sound commendably bold and enterprising, but the truth is that common courtesy, and perhaps the prospect of a good dinner, leaves them no alternative.

If the narrator is detached because he has seen too much, as the tone of the passage might suggest, then two contrary feelings – inside knowledge and a rather lofty remoteness – interestingly coexist. Perhaps the narrator feels that his general experience of India justifies his jaundiced view of the city, as it would not in the case of a more recent arrival from England. His distance from Chandrapore is marked by the fact that the city is seen in panorama rather than close-up. We also note that what catches the narrator's eye is its buildings, not its citizens.

This passage from a novel first published in 1924, when India was still under British colonial rule, is likely to sound unpleasantly condescending to a good many readers today. They might therefore be surprised to learn that Forster was a robust critic of imperialism. In fact, he was one of the most renowned liberal thinkers of his day, at a time when liberalism was in shorter supply than it is today. The novel as a whole is ambiguous in its attitude to imperial rule, but there is a good deal in it to make the enthusiasts of Empire feel distinctly uncomfortable. Forster himself worked for the Red Cross for three years in the Egyptian seaport of Alexandria, where he had a sexual relationship with a poor train conductor who was later unjustly imprisoned by the British colonial regime. He denounced British power in Egypt, detested Winston Churchill, abominated all forms of nationalism and was a champion of the Islamic world. All of which goes to suggest that there is a more complex relation between an author and his or her work than we might imagine. We shall be looking into this question a little later. The narrator of these lines may express Forster's own views, or he may do so in part, or not at all. We really have no way of knowing. Nor is it all that important.

There is an enormous irony in this passage, which the reader can become aware of only as he or she reads further into the book. The novel opens with a disclaimer, one which is instantly qualified: there is nothing extraordinary in Chandrapore, except for the Marabar Caves. So the Marabar Caves are indeed extraordinary; but we are told this in a throwaway sub-clause, so that the syntax has the effect of diminishing its significance. The emphasis of the sentence falls on 'the city of Chandrapore presents nothing extraordinary', rather than 'Except for the Marabar Caves'. The Caves are more fascinating than the city, but the syntax seems to suggest the opposite. The lines also have the effect of provoking our curiosity only to frustrate it. The Caves are no sooner mentioned than whisked away, which serves only to heighten our interest in them. This, once again, is typical of the paragraph's reticence and obliquity. It would not do for it to get too vulgarly excited about this local tourist attraction. Instead, it intimates its importance in a sideways, negative kind of way.

This ambiguity – are the Caves really out of the ordinary or not? – lies at the heart of *A Passage to India*. In a shadowy way, the very core of the book is distilled in its opening words – ironically, even teasingly so, since the reader cannot possibly be aware of this yet. Literary works quite often 'know' things that the reader does not know, or does not know yet, or perhaps will never know. Nobody will ever know what was in a letter written by Milly Theale to Merton Densher at the end of Henry James's novel *The Wings of the Dove*, since another character burns it before we can learn what it contains. One might say that not even Henry James knows its contents. When Shakespeare has Macbeth remind Banquo to attend a feast he is throwing, and Banquo promises to do so, the play, but not the spectator, knows that Banquo will indeed turn up for the feast; but he will attend it as a ghost, since Macbeth has had him murdered in the meantime. Shakespeare is having a little joke at the expense of his audience.

In one sense, the Marabar Caves turn out to be every bit as momentous as the opening words of the novel would suggest. They are the site of its central action. But this action may also be a non-action. Whether anything happens in the Caves is hard to decide. There are different views on the matter in the novel itself. Caves are literally hollow, so that to say that the Marabar Caves lie at the centre of the novel is to say that there is a kind of blank or void at its heart. Like many a modernist work of Forster's time, this one turns on something shadowy and elusive. It has a kind of absent centre. If there is indeed a truth at the core of the work, it seems one that is almost impossible to pin down. So the novel's opening sentence serves as a little model of the book as a whole. It asserts the significance of the Caves while syntactically playing them down, a playing down which also serves to play them up. And in doing so it foreshadows their ambiguous role in the story.

\* \* \*

We may turn now for a moment from fiction to drama. The first scene of *Macbeth* reads as follows:

1st witch: When shall we three meet again?
           In thunder, lightning, or in rain?
2nd witch: When the hurly-burly's done,
           When the battle's lost and won.
3rd witch: That will be ere the set of sun.
1st witch: Where the place?
2nd witch: Upon the heath.
3rd witch: There to meet with Macbeth.
1st witch: I come, Graymalkin.
2nd witch: Paddock calls.
3rd witch: Anon!
All: Fair is foul, and foul is fair,
   Hover through the fog and filthy air.

There are three questions asked in these thirteen lines, two of them right at the start. So the play opens on an interrogative note. In fact, *Macbeth* as a whole is awash with questions, sometimes questions responded to by another question, which helps to generate an atmosphere of uncertainty, anxiety and paranoid suspicion. To ask a question is to demand something determinate in response, but not much in this play is that, least of all the witches. As old hags with beards, it is even difficult to say what gender they belong to.

There are three of them, but they also act as one, so that in a grisly parody of the Holy Trinity it is hard to count them up as well. 'In thunder, lightning, or in rain?' also contains three items, but as the critic Frank Kermode has pointed out, the line suggests rather oddly that these kinds of weather are alternatives (there are commas between the words to point this up), whereas in fact they usually occur together in what we call a storm. So counting is a problem here too.

Questions seek for certainty and clear distinctions, but the witches confound all assured truths. They garble definitions and turn polarities on their head. Hence 'fair is foul, and foul is fair'. Or take the phrase 'hurly-burly', which means any boisterous form of activity. 'Hurly' sounds like 'burly' but is not the same, so the term contains an interplay of difference and identity. And this reflects the Unholy Trinity of the witches themselves. The same is true of 'When the battle's lost and won'. This presumably means 'lost by one army and won by the other', but there may also be a hint that when it comes to such military adventures, winning is really losing. What victory is there in hacking thousands of enemy soldiers to death?

Lost and won are opposites, but the 'and' between them (technically known as a copula) puts them on the same level, thus making them sound the same; so that once again we have a confusion of identity and otherness. It is as though we are forced to hold in our heads the contradiction that a thing can be both itself and something else. In the end, this will be true for Macbeth of human existence, which looks vital and positive enough but is really a kind of nullity. It is 'a tale told by an idiot, full of sound and fury, signifying nothing'. Nothing is, he remarks, but what is not. Nothing, and how it is only a hair's breadth away from something, is a central issue in Shakespeare. Rarely has there been so much ado about nothing in the annals of world literature.

The witches will turn out to be prophets who can foresee the future. Perhaps this is already clear from these opening lines, when the second witch declares that the three of them will meet again when the battle is over. But maybe this involves no pre-vision at all; maybe they have already arranged to meet then, and the first witch simply needs reminding of the fact. The third witch remarks that the battle will be over before sunset, but this, too, may require no precognitive powers. Battles are generally over before sunset. There is not much point in fighting an enemy you can't see. One might expect the three weird sisters, as Macbeth will later call them, to be able to predict the outcome of the contest, but they do not. 'Lost and won', which is true of almost all battles, may be a canny way of hedging their bets in this respect. So it is not clear whether the women are prophesying or not. Their foretelling of the future is not to be trusted, as Macbeth will discover to his cost. Their prophetic utterances are ridden with paradox and ambiguity, but so also is the question of whether they are making such claims. Ambiguity can be enriching, as all students of literature are aware, but it can also be lethal, as the hero will discover.

Next in line is the Almighty. The first line of the Bible reads: 'In the beginning, God created the heavens and the earth.' It is a magnificently resonant opening to the most celebrated text in the world, simple and authoritative at the same time. The phrase 'In the beginning' refers, of course, to the beginning of the world. Grammatically speaking, it would be possible to read it as concerning God's own beginning, meaning that creating the world was the very first thing he got up to. The Creation was the first item on the divine agenda, before God went on to organise dreadful weather for the English and in a calamitous lapse of attention allowed Michael Jackson to slip into existence. But since God by definition has no origin, this cannot be the case. We are talking about the source of the universe, not about the genealogy of God himself. Since this statement is also the first line of the text, however, it cannot help bringing this fact to mind as well. The beginning of the Bible is about the beginning. The work and the world seem for a moment to coincide.

The narrator of Genesis uses the phrase 'In the beginning' because, like 'once upon a time', it is a time-honoured way of starting a story. Roughly speaking, 'once upon a time' is how fairy tales begin, whereas 'In the beginning' is how myths of origin begin. There are many such myths among the cultures of the world, of which the first chapter of the Bible is one. A good many literary works are set in the past, but it is hard to get more back-dated than the Book of Genesis. To step any further back would be to fall off the edge. The verbal gesture 'Once upon a time' pushes a fable so far off from the present into some misty mytho-logical realm that it no longer seems to belong to human history. It deliberately avoids locating the story in a specific place or time, thus lending it an aura of timelessness and universality. We might be less enraptured by 'Little Red Riding Hood' if it were to inform us that Little Red Riding Hood had a Master's degree from Berkeley, or that the Wolf had spent some time incarcerated in a Bangkok penitentiary. 'Once upon a time' signals to the reader not to raise certain questions, such as Is this true? Where did it happen? Was it before or after the invention of cornflakes?

In a similar way, the formulaic phrase 'In the beginning' instructs us not to ask at what point in time this event took place, since it means among other things 'At the beginning of time itself', and it is difficult to see how time itself could have begun at a specific time. It is hard to imagine the universe being created at precisely 3.17 p.m. on a Wednesday. In the same way, it is odd to say, as people sometimes do, that eternity will begin when they die. Eternity cannot begin. People might move from time to eternity, but this could not be an event in eternity. There are no events in eternity.

There is, however, a problem with this splendid opening line, which tells us that God created the universe in the beginning. But how could he not have done? He can't have created it halfway through. To say that something was created in the beginning is to say that it originated at the origin. It is a kind of tautology. So the first three words of the Bible could be lopped off with no great loss of sense. Perhaps whoever wrote them imagined that time began at a certain point, and when it did so God created the universe. But we know today that there would be no time without the universe. Time and the universe sprang into being simultaneously.

The Book of Genesis sees God's act of creation as a plucking of order from chaos. At first things were dark and void, but then God lent them shape and substance. In this sense, the story reverses the usual sequence of a narrative. A good many narratives begin with some semblance of order, which is then somehow disrupted. If there were not some shake-up or dislocation, the story would never get off the ground. Without the arrival of Mr Darcy, Elizabeth Bennet of Jane Austen's *Pride and Prejudice* might have stayed perpetually unmarried. Oliver Twist might never have encountered Fagin if he hadn't asked for more, and Hamlet might have come to a less sticky end had he stuck to his studies in Wittenberg.

There is another opening sentence in the Bible which rivals the first line of Genesis for rhetorical splendour. We find it at the beginning of St John's Gospel: 'In the beginning was the Word, and the Word was with God, and the Word was God.' 'In the beginning was the Word' is an allusion to the second person of the Trinity; but because it crops up at the start of a passage of prose, we cannot help thinking of this beginning as well, which is also a matter of words. These are first words about the first Word. As with the first line of Genesis, the text and what it talks about seem momentarily to mirror one another. Note also the dramatic effect of the syntax. The sentence is an example of what is technically known as parataxis, in which a writer strings clauses together without indicating how they are to be co-ordinated with or subordinated to each other. (You find this device in a lot of sub-Hemingwayesque American writing: 'He passed Rico's bar and turned towards the square and saw there were still a few stragglers left over from the carnival and felt the sour taste of last night's whisky still in his mouth . . .') Parataxis risks a certain flatness, dead-levelling the clauses of a sentence so that there is little variation of tone. St John's words, however, avoid this monotony by offering themselves as a little narrative in which we are eager to know what comes next.

As in all good narratives, there is a surprise in store for us at the end. We learn that the Word was in the beginning, then that it was with God, and then, quite unexpectedly, that the Word *was* God. This has something of the unsettling effect of 'Fred was with his uncle, and Fred was his uncle.' How can the Word be with God but also be God? As with the Macbeth witches, we are presented with a paradox of difference and identity. In the beginning was the paradox, the unthinkable, that which defeats language – which is to say that this particular Word is beyond the grasp of merely human words. The surprise is underlined by the syntax. The phrases 'In the beginning was the Word' and 'and the Word was with God' are the same length (six words each) and have the same kind of rhythmical pattern; so we are probably anticipating another such phrase to balance them – say, 'and the Word shone forth in truth'. Instead, we get the abrupt 'and the Word was God'. It is as though the line sacrifices its rhythmical poise to the power of this revelation. The first two flowing phrases build up to a terse, flat, emphatic announcement, one which sounds as though it is not to be argued with. Syntactically speaking, the sentence ends with a kind of let-down, undercutting our expectation of some final rhetorical flourish. Semantically speaking, however (semantics being concerned with questions of meaning), its conclusion packs a formidable punch.

One of the most renowned opening sentences in English litera-ture reads as follows: 'It is a truth universally acknowledged, that a single man in possession of a good fortune must be in want of a wife.' This, the first sentence of Jane Austen's *Pride and Prejudice,* is generally regarded as a small masterpiece of irony, though the irony does not exactly leap from the page. It lies in the difference between what is said – that everyone agrees that rich men need wives – and what is plainly meant, which is that this assumption is mostly to be found among unmarried women in search of a well-heeled husband. In an ironic reversal, the desire which the sentence ascribes to wealthy bachelors is actually one felt by needy spinsters.

A rich man's need for a wife is presented as a universal truth, which makes it sound as unarguable as a geometrical theorem. It is presented almost as a fact of Nature. If it is indeed a fact of Nature, then unmarried women are not to be blamed for thrusting them-selves forward as these men's prospective partners. It is simply the way of the world. They are merely responding to what pros-perous bachelors want. Austen's scrupulously diplomatic words thus exonerate young unmarried woman and their pushy mothers from the charge of greed or social climbing. They draw a veil of decorum over these disreputable motives. But the sentence also allows us to see it doing this, which is where the irony lurks. People, it suggests, feel better about their own baser desires if they can rationalise them as part of the natural order of things. There is a certain amusement to be reaped from watching them engage in this bad faith. The language of the sentence, abstract, beautifully measured and slightly dry in Austen's familiar manner, needs this mild irony to enliven it a little. One sign that this is not modern English is the comma after 'acknowledged', which would not be thought necessary in a modern text.

Austen's irony can be tart and pointed, as can some of her moral judgements. Not many authors would suggest, as she does in *Persuasion*, that one of her characters would have been better off never being born. It is hard to get tarter than that. The irony which opens *Pride and Prejudice*, by contrast, is delightfully bland, as is the one encoded in the first lines of Geoffrey Chaucer's Prologue to his *Canterbury Tales*:

> *Whan that April with his showres soote*
> *The droughte of March hath perced to the roote,*
> *And bathed every veyne in swich licour,*
> *Of which vertu engendred is the flowr;*
> *Whan Zephyrus eek with his sweete breeth*
> *Inspired hath in every holt and heath*
> *The tendre croppes, and the yonge sonne*
> *Hath in the Ram his halve cours yronne,*
> *And smale fowles maken melodye*
> *That sleepen al the night with open ye –*
> *So priketh hem Nature in hir corages –*
> *Thanne longen folk to goon on pilgramages . . .*

When spring renews the earth, men and women feel the same sap stirring in their blood, which is part of what inspires them to go on pilgrimage. There is a secret affinity between Nature's beneficent cycles and the human spirit. But people also make pilgrimages in spring because the weather is likely to be good. They might be less keen to trek all the way to Canterbury in the depths of winter. Chaucer begins his great poem, then, by paying homage to humanity at the very moment he cuts it satirically down to size. People go on pilgrimage because they are morally frail, and one sign of this frailty is that they prefer to travel at a time of year when they won't get frozen to the marrow.

If the first sentence of *Pride and Prejudice* is legendary, there are some equally celebrated first words in American literature: 'Call me Ishmael.' (It has been suggested that this statement could be modernised by the simple addition of a comma: 'Call me, Ishmael.') This laconic opening sentence of Melville's *Moby-Dick* is hardly a foretaste of what is to come, since the novel as a whole is famous for its ornate, mouth-filling literary style. The sentence is also mildly ironic, since only one character in the novel ever does call the narrator Ishmael. Why, however, should he invite the reader to do so? Because it is his actual name, or because of the name's symbolic connotations? The biblical Ishmael, the son of Abraham by his Egyptian servant Hagar, was an exile, outlaw and wanderer. So perhaps Ishmael is an appropriate pseudonym for this seasoned traveller of the deep. Or is it that the narrator wants to conceal his real name from us? And if so, why? Does his apparent openness (he begins by amicably inviting us to use his first name, if indeed it is a first name) cloak a mystery?

People called Maria do not usually say 'Call me Maria.' They say 'My name is Maria.' To say 'Call me X' is generally a request to be called by a nickname, as in 'My real name is Algernon Digby-Stuart, but you can call me Lulu.' One normally does this for the convenience of others. It would sound strange to say 'My real name is Doris, but you can call me Quentin Clarence Esterhazy the Third.' 'Ishmael', however, doesn't sound like much of a nickname. So one assumes that it is either the narrator's real name, or that it is a pseudonym he has chosen to signify his status as a wandering outcast. If this is the case, then he is concealing his actual name from us, and doing so just at the moment when he seems most intimate and inviting. The fact that the Western world is not exactly stuffed to the rafters with people called Ishmael, as opposed to people called Doris, seems to confirm the point.

'Call me Ishmael' is an address to the reader, and like all such addresses it gives the fictional game away. Simply to acknowledge the presence of a reader is to confess that this is a novel, which realist novels are usually reluctant to do. They generally try to pretend that they are not novels at all but true-life reports. To recognise the existence of a reader is to risk ruining their air of reality. Whether *Moby-Dick* is an unqualifiedly realist work is another question, but it is realist for enough of the time to make this opening gambit untypical of the book as a whole. For a novelist to write 'Dear reader, take pity on this poor blundering fool of a country doctor' is implicitly to admit in the phrase 'Dear reader' that there is no actual country doctor at all, blundering or otherwise – that this is a piece of verbal artifice, not a slice of rural life. In which case we might well be less inclined to pity the foolish doctor than if we knew or supposed that he was real. (Some literary theorists, incidentally, hold that you cannot really pity, admire, fear or abhor a fictional character, but can only 'fictionally' experience such emotions. People who cling white-faced to each other while watching horror movies are fictionally, not genuinely, afraid. This, too, is another question.)

Since 'Ishmael' sounds more like a literary name than a real one, this may be another signal that we are in the presence of fiction. On the other hand, the name may sound fictional because it is not the narrator's real name but a pseudonym. Perhaps his real name is Fred Worm, and he has chosen this more exotic title to compensate for the fact. If he is not really called Ishmael, the reader might wonder what his real name is. But if we are not given his real name, then he does not have one. It is not as though Melville is concealing it. You cannot conceal something that does not exist. All that exists of Ishmael as a character is a set of black marks on a page. It would not make sense, for example, to claim that he has a scar on his forehead but that the novel fails to mention it. If the novel does not mention it, then it does not exist. A piece of fiction may tell us that one of its characters is concealing his or her real name under a pseudonym; but even if we are actually given the name, it is as much part of the fiction as the pseudonym itself. Charles Dickens's last novel, *The Mystery of Edwin Drood*, contains a character who is clearly in disguise, and who may well be someone we have encountered elsewhere in the book. But since Dickens died before completing the work, we shall never know what face the disguise is concealing. It is true that there is someone beneath the disguise, but not that it is anyone in particular.

* * *

Let us turn again for a while to poetry, taking the beginning of six well-known poems. The first is the opening line of John Keats's 'To Autumn': 'Season of mists and mellow fruitfulness'. What strikes one about the line is the sheer opulence of its sound-texture. It is as

25

scrupulously orchestrated as a symphonic chord, full of rustling *s* sounds and murmuring *m*s. Everything is sibilant and mellifluous, with scarcely any hard or sharp consonants. The *f*s of 'fruitfulness' might seem an exception, but it is softened by the *r* which is pronounced along with it. There is a rich tapestry of sound here, full of parallelisms and subtle variations. The *m* of 'mists' is reflected in the *m* of 'mellow', the *f* of 'of' is echoed in the *f* of 'fruitfulness', the *s* sounds of 'mists' is picked up again in the 'ness' of 'fruitfulness', while the *e* of 'Season', the *i* of 'mists' and the *e* of 'mellow' form an intricate pattern of sameness and difference.

The sheer packedness of the line also arrests the eye. It manages to cram in as many syllables as it can without becoming cloying or sickly sweet. This sensuous richness is meant to evoke the ripeness of autumn, so that the language seems to become part of what it speaks of. The line is plumped full of meaning, so it is not surprising that the poem goes on to discuss autumn itself in precisely these terms:

> To bend with apples the mossed cottage-trees,
>     And fill all fruit with ripeness to the core;
>         To swell the gourd, and plump the hazel shells
>     With a sweet kernel; to set budding more,
> And still more, later flowers for the bees,
> Until they think warm days will never cease,
>         For Summer has o'er-brimmed their clammy cells.

Perhaps the poem, however unwittingly, is talking about itself here in the act of depicting the figure of Autumn. It itself avoids being clammy and overbrimmed, though it is prepared to run the risk of being so. Like autumn, it is poised at a point where maturity might always pass over into an oppressive surplus (of growth in the case of autumn, and language in the case of the poem). But it is held back from such distasteful excess by some inner restraint.

A later English writer, Philip Larkin, also writes about natural growth in his poem 'The Trees':

*The trees are coming into leaf*
*Like something almost being said . . .*

This is a daringly upfront kind of image for the usually downbeat Larkin. It sees the burgeoning leaves as like words almost at the point of articulation. Yet there is a sense in which the image undoes itself. When the trees come fully into leaf, it will no longer hold true. It is not as though the trees are murmuring now and will be shouting then. We might think of a tree striving to come into blossom as akin to someone trying to say something. But we are unlikely to imagine a tree in full leaf as an articulate statement. So the simile is true now, but will cease to apply later, when the whole process is complete. One of the striking aspects of the lines is the way they make us see a tree, with its pattern of twigs, leaves and branches, as a visual image of the invisible roots of language. It is as though the processes underlying our speech are X-rayed, materialised, projected into visual terms.

An even more celebrated Larkin poem, 'The Whitsun Weddings', begins like this:

*That Whitsun, I was late getting away:*
*    Not till about*
*One-twenty on the sunlit Saturday*
*Did my three-quarters-empty train pull out . . .*

The first line, an iambic pentameter, is calculatedly flat, casual and colloquial. Nobody would guess that this was poetry if they were to stumble on it out of context. As though aware of this, however, the poem makes an instant counter-move. 'Not till about' is a half-line, where we were expecting a complete pentameter. It represents a sudden, adroit manipulation of the metre which signals 'Yes, this is indeed poetry, although you might not have thought so a couple of seconds ago.' What else in the lines intimates this? The rhymes, which run counter to the studied ordinariness of the language and lend it some discreet shape. This is art after all, even though it is partly intent on suppressing the fact. The reserved middle-class Englishman does not put his artistry on show in the manner of some dandyish Parisian aesthete, any more than he boasts of his bank balance or sexual prowess.

Critics are always on the hunt for ambiguities, and there is a notable one in the first line of an Emily Dickinson verse: 'My life closed twice before it's close.' Dickinson writes 'it's' – a grocer's apostrophe, as we might call it today – rather than 'its' because her punctuation was somewhat erratic. She also spelt 'upon' as 'opon'. It is always reassuring to discover that great writers are as fallible as oneself. W.B. Yeats once failed to obtain an academic post in Dublin because he misspelt the word 'professor' on his application.

Tenses can play some strange tricks. Dickinson's line presumably means something like 'Before I die, I shall have had two experiences doleful and devastating enough to be comparable to death itself.' But how does she know that there will have been only two, since she is not yet dead? The verb of the statement ('closed') is in the past tense because these two moments of loss have already taken place; but the effect of this is to make the poet's death seem as though it has already taken place as well. It would be too clumsy to write 'Before my life ends, it will already have ended twice', even though this is probably what the line means. There is thus a curious sense of Dickinson addressing us from the grave. If she knows that there were only two metaphorical deaths in her life, then she must be already dead, or at least on her deathbed. The dead are those to whom nothing more can happen. They are entirely event-free. Yet writing and death are incompatible. So Dickinson cannot be dead, even though she writes as though she is.

Another stunning opening in American literature is the superb first lines of Robert Lowell's poem 'The Quaker Graveyard in Nantucket':

> *A brackish reach of shoal off Madaket*
> *The sea was still breaking violently and night*
> *Had steamed into our North Atlantic Fleet,*
> *When the drowned sailor clutched the drag-net. Light*
> *Flashed from his matted head and marble feet,*
> *He grappled at the net*
> *With the coiled, hurdling muscles of his thighs . . .*

The first line of this is extraordinarily mouth-filling. To read it out loud, with its harsh vowels and stabbing consonants, is rather like chewing a piece of steak. The place-name 'Madaket' is perfect for the gritty, sinewy language of the piece. It is the kind of language that reflects the raw material environment it portrays. 'The sea was still breaking violently and night' would be a fairly regular iambic pentameter if it wasn't for the word 'still', which ruffles the metrical pattern. But the poem doesn't want smoothness or symmetry, as its syntax makes clear as well:

*The sea was still breaking violently and night*
*Had steamed into our North Atlantic Fleet,*
*When the drowned sailor clutched the drag-net. Light*
*Flashed from his matted head and marble feet . . .*

There is a violent breaking in the verse here as well as in the ocean. In a bold gesture, the third line ends a sentence and begins a new one with only one word to go. I say 'only one word to go' because the metre dictates that the line can stretch to only one more monosyllable. So Lowell audaciously begins a new sentence with the abrupt word 'Light' just as he is running out of line. As a result, we have a full stop after 'drag-net', which signals a brief but complete pause; then 'Light'; then we have to pause fractionally again, leaving the word 'Light' dangling, as we run up against the line-ending and step across to the beginning of the next line. The syntax and the metrical pattern are played off against each other to produce some memorable dramatic effects.

We may also note the curious inversion of 'night / Had steamed into our North Atlantic Fleet'. It would be more conventional to speak of the fleet steaming into the night; as it is, the night is made to sound like a vessel itself, one which is perhaps about to cause a collision. (There are similar inversions in Shakespeare – 'His coward lips did from their colour fly,' for example, an image from *Julius Caesar* which is really too cerebral and contrived to be convincing.) 'Hurdling' in 'coiled, hurdling muscles' presumably means 'like those of a hurdler'. But the phrase could also apply to the packed, hard, knotted language of the poem itself.

Literary beginnings are not always what they seem. Take, for example, the magnificent opening lines of John Milton's *Lycidas*, a poem written in memory of his fellow poet Edward King, who was drowned at sea and is the Lycidas of the piece:

> *Yet once more, O ye laurels and once more*
> *Ye myrtles brown, with ivy never sere,*
> *I come to pluck your berries harsh and crude,*
> *And with forced fingers rude,*
> *Shatter your leaves before the mellowing year.*
> *Bitter constraint, and sad occasion dear,*
> *Compels me to disturb your season due;*
> *For Lycidas is dead, dead ere his prime,*
> *Young Lycidas, and hath not left his peer:*
> *Who would not sing for Lycidas? He knew*
> *Himself to sing, and build the lofty rhyme.*
> *He must not float upon his wat'ry bier*
> *Unwept, and welter to the parching wind,*
> *Without the meed of some melodious tear.*

The name 'Lycidas' tolls dolefully through these lines like a funeral bell. In fact, these opening words are full of echoes and repetitions: 'Yet once more . . . and once more', 'dead, dead ere his prime', 'Who would not sing . . . He knew Himself to sing'. This generates a ritual or ceremonial effect, appropriately enough for a poem which is more of a public performance than a grief-stricken cry from the heart. Milton probably did not know King all that well, and there is no reason to suppose that he felt in the least agonised by his early death. In any case, King was a Royalist, while Milton himself would later become a doughty apologist for the execution of Charles I. The dead man was also training to be a cleric, whereas *Lycidas* goes on to deliver a violent attack on the established church, a perilous business at the time. No doubt this is why Milton signed the poem with his initials only.

In fact, in their coded way, these sombre lines may express a certain weary reluctance as much as melancholy. When Milton speaks of having to pluck the unripe berries of the laurel and myrtle, emblems of the poet, he means that he has been constrained to break off his spiritual preparations for becoming a great poet in order to compose this elegy. This is why the fingers that pluck the berries are forced, not free. It is also why they are rude, in the sense of not yet skilled enough at writing. In fact, the poise and authority of the lines which make this claim are more than enough to refute it. Far from being rude verse, this is highly sophisticated stuff. So weighty does Milton feel the burden of duty placed upon him that the verse makes it sound as though he is being compelled twice over, as 'bitter constraint' 'compels' him to take up his pen. The 'sad occasion dear' is, of course, the death of King, but one wonders whether Milton is not also thinking of his own frustration at having to emerge from spiritual hibernation in order to honour a colleague. It is as though he manages to turn a grumble into a tribute.

There is a parallel between King's premature death and the prematurity of the poem itself, signified by the 'berries harsh and crude'. Milton is having to fashion his lament out of materials that have not yet matured. It is as though he is projecting on to the laurel and myrtle his own sense of unripeness as a poet. Perhaps he would not be penning this masterpiece at all unless he felt he had to. It is a question of duty, not spontaneity. In this light, 'Who would not sing for Lycidas?' is solemnly disingenuous. John Milton, for one, might be a candid response. And is it really true that King, hardly the greatest bard in Christendom, did not have a peer as a poet? Once again, what about John Milton? These statements are just a standard piece of hyperbole. We are not expected to take them as burningly sincere. It is true that 'He must not float upon his wat'ry bier / Unwept, and welter to the parching wind' sounds tender enough. (Daringly, these lines get away with no fewer than four *w* sounds, without one feeling that this is excessive.) But the statement might also suggest rather less tenderly that somebody is going to have to mourn for King, so Milton had better do so himself.

The image of the watery bier, incidentally, is extraordinarily powerful. As critics have pointed out, it evokes the terrible vision of a man being tossed around in water yet dying of thirst ('parching wind'). The 'melodious tear', a bold enough image since tears do not pipe or warble, is a matter of weeping for Lycidas, bestowing a poem on him, but also of giving him water. There is something slightly odd about this last sense of the phrase, since lack of water is usually the last of a drowned man's problems. 'Meed' here means a tribute, but it can also mean a reward, which would suggest rather bizarrely that the poem is offered to King by way of recompense for his death. One assumes it is the first sense of the word that the poet has in mind.

The fact that Milton may be writing a touch reluctantly is neither here nor there. A poet can compose an authentic lament without feeling in the least distraught, just as he or she can write about love without feeling in the least amorous. Milton's lines are moving, even if the poet himself is not moved. Or not moved, at least, by King's early death. One suspects that he is more perturbed by the prospect that he himself may also be cut off in his prime, before he has a chance to become the great poet he aspires to be. Both the prematurity of King's death and the supposed immaturity of Milton as a poet are reminders of this alarming possibility. He too will be 'plucked' in the end, perhaps before his time, as he now plucks the berries to mourn the unseasonableness of his colleague's death. To pluck a plant is to inflict a kind of death on it, even if one does so in the cause of art, and thus of the living.

Milton produces *Lycidas* as one might attend the funeral service of a colleague for whom one had no particular affection. There is no hypocrisy here. On the contrary, it would be hypocritical to pretend to a grief one did not feel. In attending the funeral of an acquaintance, we are expected to feel the sentiments proper to the procedures of the ceremony itself. In a similar way, Milton's feelings in this poem are bound up with its verbal strategies. They do not consist of some heartache that lurks behind it. Post-Romantics like ourselves tend to suspect that emotion is one thing and convention another. Genuine feeling means throwing off the artifice of social forms and speaking directly from the heart. But this is probably not how Milton would have thought, or how many a non-Western culture would think today.

Nor would it have been the view of Jane Austen. For her, as for neo-classical authors in general, authentic feeling had its appropriate forms of public expression, which were regulated by social convention. To say 'convention', a word which literally means 'coming together', is to say that how I behave emotionally is not just up to me. My emotions are not my private property, as a more individualist society than Milton's or Austen's might suppose. On the contrary, there is a sense in which I learn my emotional behaviour by participating in a common culture. Syrians do not lament in the same way that the Scottish do. Convention and propriety run very deep. For Austen, propriety means not just eating your banana with a knife and fork, but conducting yourself sensitively and respectfully toward others. Civility involves more than not spitting in the sherry decanter. It also means not being boorish, arrogant, selfish and conceited.

Convention does not necessarily stifle feeling. It may judge that an emotional response is too extravagant, but also that it is too meagre. Whether one believes that sentiments and conventions are bound together, or that they are at daggers drawn, is a bone of contention between Hamlet and Claudius at the start of Shakespeare's play. Hamlet holds in his individualist way that emotions like grief should disregard the social forms, whereas Claudius takes the view that feeling and form should be on more intimate terms than this. It is also part of the difference between Eleanor and Marianne Dashwood in Austen's *Sense and Sensibility*. Poetry is a good example of how feeling and form are not necessarily at loggerheads. Form may heighten feeling as well as suppress it. *Lycidas* is not the expression of Milton's regret at the death of King. Rather, it *is* his regret. It is the kind of dutiful, ceremonious elegy appropriate in the circumstances. There is no question of insincerity, any more than it is insincere for me to wish you good morning when I have many more pressing issues on my mind than the kind of morning you might be about to have.

* * *

Perhaps the best-known play of the twentieth century, Samuel Beckett's *Waiting for Godot*, opens with the following bleak line: 'Nothing to be done.' The words are spoken by Estragon, whose companion in utter tedium and unassuaged misery is Vladimir. The most celebrated figure of that name in the twentieth century was Vladimir Lenin, who wrote a revolutionary tract entitled *What is to be Done?* This may be no more than coincidence, though not much in Beckett's writing is less than meticulously calculated. If the allusion is intentional, then it may be that the line is handed to Estragon rather than Vladimir to make it appear less obvious. It is possible, then, that a piece of drama that is generally considered to spurn history and politics in order to portray a timeless human condition actually opens with a discreet allusion to one of the most momentous of all modern political events, the Bolshevik Revolution.

This would not, in fact, be all that astonishing, since Beckett himself was by no means a non-political figure. He fought bravely for the French Resistance during the Second World War, and was later honoured for his courage by the French government. At one point he escaped by the skin of his teeth from being captured by the Gestapo, along with his equally intrepid wife. One aspect of his work that is not quite universal is his humour, which in its bathos, poker-faced pedantry, mordant wit, dark satirical edge and surreal flights of fantasy has a distinctively Irish quality to it. When the Dublin-born Beckett was asked by a Parisian journalist whether he was English, he replied, 'On the contrary.'

Another piece of fiction to which Irishness is relevant is Flann O'Brien's great novel *The Third Policeman*. It opens with these chilling words:

Not everybody knows how I killed old Phillip Mathers, smashing his jaw in with my spade; but first it is better to speak of my friendship with John Divney because it was he who first knocked old Mathers down by giving him a great blow in the neck with a special bicycle-pump which he manufactured himself out of a hollow iron bar. Divney was a strong civil man but he was lazy and idle-minded. He was personally responsible for the whole idea in the first place. It was he who told me to bring my spade.

He was the one who gave the orders on the occasion and also the explanations when they were called for.

I was born a long time ago. My father was a strong farmer and my mother owned a public house . . .

If the English of this passage reads slightly strangely, it may be partly because O'Brien was a fluent Irish speaker who wrote some of his work in the Irish language. So he is not exactly writing here in his native tongue, though he spoke English at least as well as Winston Churchill. Hiberno-English, as the kind of English spoken in Ireland is known, sometimes gives an unfamiliar twist to standard English speech, and is thus a fertile medium for generating literary effects. The name 'Mathers', for example, is pronounced in Ireland as 'Ma-hers', as 'th' behaves differently in Irish than in English. 'I was born a long time ago' is an unusual way of saying 'I am old', and a wonderfully improved one at that. The phrase 'strong farmer' in Ireland means not a muscular one but one furnished with a large number of acres.

The language of these lines is as far from the opening of *A Passage to India* as one could imagine. Whereas Forster's prose is suave and civilised, O'Brien's is apparently artless and unadorned. There is a roughness about the prose, as there is about the characters it presents. The rambling first sentence, which stretches over several lines, is a case in point. It contains a number of distinct segments but only two punctuation marks, which gives the effect of a narrator who is growling or muttering his random thoughts out loud. I say 'random' because there is something oddly inconsequential about a sentence like 'Divney was a strong civil man but he was lazy and idle-minded.' The fact that he was lazy and idle-minded does not seem to have much of a bearing on the matter in hand. Indeed, the passage makes him sound reasonably active and well organised, so perhaps this is an unmerited put-down on the narrator's part. We assume that the narrator is a man, by the way, partly because men are more likely to commit murder than women; partly because when women do kill, they are unlikely to do so by smashing in their victim's jaw with a spade; and partly because the narrator and Divney sound like long-standing male cronies. Male authors also tend to favour male narrators. But all this could be presumptuous.

Artlessness of this kind demands a good deal of art. O'Brien's prose has the air of being unsculptured, but the whole paragraph is meticulously set up for maximum dramatic impact. Note, for example, how the arresting effect of the opening confession ('Not everybody knows how I killed old Phillip Mathers') is reinforced by the fact that it is cast in the negative. (This, as it happens, is a work of fiction much concerned with negativity, so it is fitting that its first word should be 'Not'.) 'I killed old Phillip Mathers' would lack the shocking off-handedness of the opening sentence, which gains some of its unnerving power from letting us know that the narrator murdered Mathers while appearing to be focused on something else (the fact that not everybody is aware of it). If this is a blunt assault on the reader's sensibilities, it is also a faintly devious one. No sooner has the narrator made his momentous declaration than the sentence swerves abruptly aside from it ('but first it is better to speak of my friendship with John Divney'). This, too, is a crafty way of increasing the force of the opening announcement. The reader is left open-mouthed while the narrator moves coolly on to another topic, as though unaware of the shattering nature of what he has just revealed. There is, incidentally, something slightly strange about the phrase 'Not everybody knows how

I killed old Phillip Mathers'. 'Not everybody' suggests that more than just a few people do, which implies that the murder is to some extent public knowledge.

What the narrator moves on to is the business of excusing himself. No sooner has he confessed to smashing in Mathers's jaw than he is busy trying to pin the blame on Divney, who supposedly struck the first blow and who was 'personally responsible for the whole idea in the first place'. It is as though the narrator, who remains nameless throughout the story, is hoping that by the time we have read our way from 'It was he who told me to bring my spade' to 'the explanations when they were called for', we will have forgotten that he has just branded himself as a murderer. There is something darkly comic about this about-turn, as there is about the feeble stab at self-justification of 'It was he who told me to bring my spade.' It is hard to imagine a jury being swayed to clemency by this information. There is also something funny about the vagueness of the phrase 'and also the explanations when they were called for'. What explanations? Explanations to the narrator about why they were murdering Mathers (did he not know this already?), or explanations of how the operation should be carried out, or explanations ready to hand should the deed be discovered?

Absurdity is a familiar Irish literary mode, and there is plenty of it in these stark sentences. Why does Divney kill old Mathers with a bicycle pump, of all improbable weapons? (The novel is obsessed with bicycles.) How easy would it be to fashion a bicycle-pump out of a hollow iron bar, and why should Divney do so in the first place? The bicycle was a common mode of transport in the Ireland of the time, so there should have been no shortage of pumps. The narrator surely cannot mean that Divney turned the bar into a bicycle-pump for the express purpose of belabouring Mathers with it, though this ludicrous possibility cannot be entirely ruled out. Why not just use the bar instead? It is much more likely that Divney had adapted the bar some time earlier, but we would still like to know why. Why didn't the narrator knock the victim down with his spade and then deal him a lethal blow with it, rather than Divney striking him first and then the narrator? Could it be that the implausible tale of the bicycle-pump is just a clumsy way of deflecting guilt on to Divney, and that he actually took no part in the crime? This possibility, at least, we can exclude, since when we read further into the book we shall discover that Divney did indeed wield his bicycle-pump to lay Mathers low. (When he does so, incidentally, the narrator overhears the old man 'say something softly in a conversational tone' as he collapses to the ground, words which sound rather like 'I do not care for celery' or 'I left my glasses in the scullery'.)

The opening of *The Third Policeman* is gripping enough, but it would be hard to imagine a more eye-catching first sentence than that of Anthony Burgess's novel *Earthly Powers*: 'It was the afternoon of my eighty-first birthday, and I was in bed with my catamite when Ali announced that the archbishop had come to see me.' (A catamite is a man's boy lover.) In the span of a single sentence, the novel sets a deliciously scandalous scene: an eighty-one-year-old man in bed with a boy, yet a man distinguished and respectable enough to have a servant (we assume this is what Ali is), and to be worthy of a visit from an archbishop. He is also cultivated enough to use the word 'catamite', which is not often to be heard on Fox TV. The fact that he seems unembarrassed by his situation might suggest a certain English sangfroid. One of the achievements of the sentence is the off-hand, economical way it supplies the reader in one fell swoop with all this information, without the slightest sense of being verbally overpopulated. Since Ali is a foreign name, we might also assume that we are in some suitably exotic overseas setting. It is also part of the Western stereotype of the East that catamites are in greater supply there than in Leeds or Long Island. Perhaps we suspect that the narrator is a colonial official of some kind, illicitly making use of the local amenities.

We will soon learn, in fact, that he is a celebrated writer. In fact, he is modelled on the English author W. Somerset Maugham, who was once described as 'one of the stately homos of England'. This opening sentence is a wicked parody of Maugham's style – though, as one critic has suggested, it is a parody superior to anything Maugham ever managed to produce himself. The copy outshines the original, rather as the word 'Vienna' is more poetic than 'Wien'. The novel's first sentence, then, is supposed to be written by a novelist, which gives us a clue to the entire affair. The narrator is trying to come up with the kind of opening literary gambit that will outdo all others in sheer sensationalism. So there is a sense in which this initial declaration is secretly about itself.

Part of the joke, however, is that it is not meant to be invented purely for literary effect (though it is, of course, invented, by Anthony Burgess himself). The reader is supposed to take it as an account of an actual situation. Which is to say that the narrator, who writes novels, also lives the kind of colourfully dissipated life one might come across only in a novel. It is here that the interplay of fiction and reality become truly dizzying. The narrator, who is a novelist, behaves like a character in a novel – which, as it happens, is exactly what he is. Yet though he is a fictional figure, he is based on a real one. However, the author on whom he is based (Somerset Maugham) seemed to many observers to be a touch unreal. At this point the reader may feel like falling into bed, with or without a catamite.

There is scarcely a word in this scurrilous first sentence that is not designed to raise the reader's eyebrows. In the opening sentence of George Orwell's *1984*, by contrast, only one word is intended to do so:

It was a bright cold day in April, and the clocks were striking thirteen. Winston Smith, his chin nuzzled into his breast in an effort to escape the vile wind, slipped quickly through the glass doors of Victory Mansions, though not quickly enough to prevent a swirl of gritty dust from entering along with him.

The first sentence gains its effect from carefully dropping the word 'thirteen' into an otherwise unremarkable piece of description, thus signalling that the scene is set either in some unfamiliar civilisation or in the future. Some things haven't changed (the month is still named April, and winds can still be bitter), but others have, and part of the effect of the sentence springs from this juxtaposition of the ordinary and the unfamiliar. Most readers who open Orwell's novel will know already that it is set in the future, though in the author's future rather than our own. One might feel, however, that the strangely striking clocks are a little too *voulu*, a term meaning 'willed' in French that is used to describe an effect that is rather too calculated or self-conscious. Perhaps this detail is too contrivedly placed. It proclaims 'This is science fiction' rather too loudly.

This is a dystopian novel (dystopia being the opposite of utopia) about an all-powerful state that can manipulate everything from the historical past to its citizens' habits of mind. No doubt it is this state that gave Victory Mansions its triumphalistic name. Yet it may be that the second sentence of the passage offers a mild degree of hope in this dismal situation. As Winston Smith enters the Mansions, a swirl of gritty dust manages to infiltrate the building along with him; and though the novel itself seems to find some ominous meaning in this intrusion (the wind is 'vile'), a reader might find this gust of grit rather less sinister. Dust and grit are signs of the random and accidental. They represent bits of stuff without rhyme or reason, which fail to add up to any total or meaningful design. One might therefore see them as the opposite of the totalitarian regime portrayed by the novel. In the same way, the wind might be seen as a force that defies human regulation. It blows as it will, now this way and now the other. There is no rhyme or reason to it, either. The state, it would appear, has at least not been able to harness Nature to its purposes. And totalitarian states are uneasy with anything they cannot dragoon into order and intelligibility. Perhaps the regime cannot entirely banish chance, rather as Victory Mansions cannot entirely keep out the dust.

Some readers will no doubt find this interpretation absurdly fanciful. This is because it may well be exactly that. It seems improbable that Orwell himself intended the dust as a positive image, or that the thought even crossed his mind. But we shall see later that readers must not always meekly conform to what they imagine an author had in mind. All the same, there may be other reasons why the interpretation does not work. It might not fit in with what we discover as we read further into the book. We might find that the wind is always presented as an image of evil. On the other hand, we might not – in which case sceptical readers might need to find some other grounds for judging this a ridiculous reading of the text, a conclusion which is by no means out of the question.

In these brief critical exercises, I have tried to show some of the various strategies literary criticism may involve. You can analyse the sound-texture of a passage, or fasten on what seem significant ambiguities, or look at the way grammar and syntax are put to work. You can examine the emotional attitudes that a passage seems to take up to what it is presenting, or focus on some revealing paradoxes, discrepancies and contradictions. Tracking down the unspoken implications of what is said can sometimes be important. Judging the tone of a passage, and how this may shift or waver, can be equally productive. It can be helpful to try to define the exact quality of a piece of writing. It may be sombre, off-hand, devious, colloquial, terse, jaded, glib, theatrical, ironic, laconic, artless, abrasive, sensuous, sinewy and so on. What all these critical strategies have in common is their heightened sensitivity to language. Even exclamation marks may be worth a few sentences of critical comment. One might call all this the 'micro' aspects of literary criticism. But there are 'macro' issues too, such as character, plot, theme, narrative and the like, and it is to these that we can now turn.

# CHAPTER 2

# Character

One of the most common ways of overlooking the 'literariness' of a play or novel is to treat its characters as though they were actual people. In one sense, to be sure, this is almost impossible to avoid. To describe Lear as bullying, irascible and self-deluded is inevitably to make him sound like some modern-day newspaper mogul. The difference between Lear and the mogul, however, is that the former is simply a pattern of black marks on a page, whereas the latter, more's the pity, is not. The mogul had an existence before we encountered him, which is not true of literary characters. Hamlet was not really a university student before the play opens, even though the play itself tells us that he was. He was nothing at all. Hedda Gabler does not exist a second before she steps on stage, and all we shall ever know about her is what Ibsen's play decides to tell us. There are no other sources of information available.

When Heathcliff disappears from Wuthering Heights for a mysterious stretch of time, the novel does not tell us where he runs off to. There is a theory that he returns to the Liverpool where he was first discovered as a child and grows rich in the slave trade there, but it is equally possible that he sets up a hairdressing salon in Reading. The truth is that he does not end up in any place on the map. Instead, he takes himself off to an indeterminate location. There are no such locations in real life, not even Gary, Indiana, but there are in fiction. We might also ask how many teeth Heathcliff has, to which the only possible answer is an indeterminate number. It is legitimate for us to infer that he has teeth, but the work does not tell us how many. A celebrated critical essay is entitled 'How Many Children had Lady Macbeth?' We can deduce from the play that she has probably given birth to at least one, but we are not told whether there are more. So Lady Macbeth has an indeterminate number of children, which may prove convenient when applying for child benefit.

Literary figures have no pre-history. It is said that a theatre director who was staging one of Harold Pinter's plays asked the playwright for some hints as to what his characters were up to before they came on stage. Pinter's reply was 'Mind your own fucking business.' Emma Woodhouse, the heroine of Jane Austen's novel *Emma*, exists only as long as somebody is reading about her. If nobody is reading about her at any given time (an unlikely eventuality, given the brilliance of the novel and the billions of English-language readers in the world), she lapses into non-existence. Emma does not survive the conclusion of *Emma*. She lives in a text, not a grand country mansion, and a text is a transaction between itself and a reader. A book is a material object which exists even if nobody picks it up, but this is not true of a text. A text is a pattern of meaning, and patterns of meaning do not lead lives of their own, like snakes or sofas.

Some Victorian novels end by peering fondly into their characters' futures, imagining them growing old, grey and gleeful among a horde of frolicsome grandchildren. They find it hard to let their characters go, as parents sometimes find it hard to let their children go. But peering fondly into one's characters' futures is, of course, simply a literary device. Literary figures do not have futures, any more than incarcerated serial killers do. Shakespeare makes this point in a beautiful passage towards the end of *The Tempest*, another part of which we have looked at already:

> *be cheerful, sir.*
> *Our revels now are ended. These our actors,*
> *As I foretold you, were all spirits, and*
> *Are melted into air, into thin air;*
> *And, like the baseless fabric of this vision,*
> *The cloud-capp'd towers, the gorgeous palaces,*
> *The solemn temples, the great globe itself,*
> *Yea, all which it inherit, shall dissolve,*
> *And, like this insubstantial pageant faded,*
> *Leave not a rack behind. We are such stuff*
> *As dreams are made on; and our little life*
> *Is rounded with a sleep . . .*

As the drama draws to a close, its characters and events vanish into thin air, since, being fictions, there is nowhere else for them to go. Their author, too, is just about to disappear from the London theatre and return home to his native Stratford. Interestingly, this speech by Prospero does not contrast the unreality of the stage with the solid, flesh-and-blood existence of real men and women. On the contrary, it seizes on the flimsiness of dramatic characters as a metaphor for the fleeting, fantasy-ridden quality of actual human lives. It is we who are made of dreams, not just such figments of Shakespeare's imagination as Ariel and Caliban. The cloud-capped towers and gorgeous palaces of this earth are mere stage scenery after all.

The theatre can teach us some truth, but it is the truth of the illusory nature of our existence. It can alert us to the dream-like quality of our lives, their brevity, mutability and lack of solid grounds. As such, by reminding us of our mortality, it can foster in us the virtue of humility. This is a precious accomplishment, since much of our moral trouble springs from the unconscious assumption that we will live for ever. In fact, our lives will meet with as categorical a conclusion as the end of *The Tempest*. This, however, may not be as dismaying as it sounds. If we were to accept that our existence is as fragile and fugitive as that of Prospero and Miranda, we might reap some advantage from doing so. We might cling to life in a less white-knuckled way, and so enjoy ourselves more and injure others less. Perhaps this is why Prospero, rather strangely in the context, urges us to be cheerful. The transience of things is not wholly to be regretted. If love and bottles of Châteauneuf-du-Pape pass away, so do wars and tyrants.

The word 'character' nowadays can mean a sign, letter or symbol as well as a literary figure. It derives from an ancient Greek term meaning a stamping tool which makes a distinctive mark. From there it came to mean the peculiar mark of an individual, rather like his signature. A character, like a character reference today, was a sign, portrait or description of what a man or woman was like. Then, after a while, it came to mean the man or woman as such. The sign that had stood for the individual became the individual herself. The distinctiveness of the mark became the uniqueness of the person. The word 'character' is thus an example of the figure of speech known as synecdoche, in which a part represents the whole.

This is of more than merely technical interest. The shift from character as the peculiar mark of an individual to character as the individual himself is bound up with a whole social history. It belongs, in a word, to the rise of modern individualism. Individuals are now defined by what is peculiar to them, such as their signature or inimitable personality. What distinguishes us from each other is more important than what we have in common. What makes Tom Sawyer Tom Sawyer is all those attributes he does not share with Huck Finn. Lady Macbeth is what she is because of her ferocious will and thrusting ambition, not because she suffers, laughs, grieves and sneezes. Since these are things she shares with the rest of her species, they do not really count as part of her character. Pressed to an extreme, this rather curious conception of men and women suggests that a great deal, perhaps most, of what they are and do is not really *them*. It is not distinctive to them; and since character or personality is thought to be incomparable, it cannot count as part of it.

Today, the term 'character' means an individual's mental and moral qualities, as in Prince Andrew's comment that being shot at during the Falklands War was 'very character-building'. Perhaps he would care to have his character built a little more often. The word also, of course, refers to figures in novels, plays, movies and the like. We still use the term of actual people, however, as in 'Who were those characters throwing up out of the Vatican window?' It can also mean a capricious or idiosyncratic individual, as in 'By God, sir, he's a character!' The phrase is interestingly used more about men than about women, and reflects a very English delight in eccentricity. The English tend to admire curmudgeonly, nonconformist types who make a point of not fitting in with their fellows. Such oddballs are agreeably incapable of being anything but themselves. People who carry a stoat on their shoulder or wear brown paper bags over their heads are said to be characters, which suggests that their aberrations are to be genially indulged. There is a spirit of tolerance about the word 'character'. It saves you from having to take certain people into protective custody.

As in the fiction of Charles Dickens, this quirkiness can range from the lovable to the downright sinister. There are also Dickens characters who hover somewhere between the two, full of amusing foibles but also faintly alarming. They seem unable to see the world from anyone's perspective but their own. This kind of moral squint makes them comic, but also potentially monstrous. There is a thin line between a vigorous independence of mind and being shut off from other people inside one's own ego. Being walled up inside oneself for too long results in a sort of insanity. 'Characters' are never far from a kind of madness, as the life of Samuel Johnson would suggest. The fascinating is only a step away from the freakish.

You cannot have a deviation without a norm. Idiosyncratic people may take pride in being stubbornly themselves, but there is a sense in which their waywardness is dependent on the existence of 'normal' men and women. What counts as eccentric depends on what is taken as standard behaviour. This, once again, is clear enough from the world of Dickens, whose figures tend to divide between the conventional and the grotesque. For every Little Nell, a dreary paragon of virtue in *The Old Curiosity Shop*, there is a Quilp, a savage dwarf in the same novel who chews lighted cigars and threatens to bite his wife. For every faceless young gent like Nicholas Nickleby there is a Wackford Squeers, the one-eyed monster of a rogue schoolmaster in the same work, who rather than teaching his downtrodden students to spell the word 'window' gets them to clean the school windows instead.

The problem is that if the normal characters have all the virtue, the freakish figures have all the life. Nobody would have an orange juice with Oliver Twist if they could share a beer with Fagin.

Roguery is more alluring than respectability. Once the Victorian middle classes had defined normality as thrift, prudence, patience, chastity, meekness, self-discipline and industriousness, the devil was clearly going to have all the best tunes. In such a situation, aberration is plainly the option to go for. Hence the postmodern obsession with vampires and Gothic horrors, the perverse and peripheral, which has become as much an orthodoxy as thrift and chastity once were. Few readers of *Paradise Lost* prefer Milton's God, who speaks like a constipated civil servant, to his smoulderingly defiant Satan. In fact, it is almost possible to pinpoint the first moment in English history at which virtue becomes boring and vice beguiling. The philosopher Thomas Hobbes, writing in the mid-seventeenth century, admires such heroic or aristocratic qualities as courage, honour, glory and magnanimity; the philosopher John Locke, writing at the end of the seventeenth century, champions the middle-class values of industry, thrift, sobriety and moderation.

Even so, it is not quite true that Dickens's grotesques transgress the norm. They certainly flout conventional forms of conduct. But they are so stuck in their ways, so compulsively consistent in their offbeatness, that they come to represent norms in themselves. They are as much prisoners of their own outlandish habits as the respectable characters are prisoners of convention. We are presented with a society in which everyone is his or her own measure. Everyone just does his own thing, whether it consists of biting his wife or jingling the change in his pockets. This, however, is as far from authentic freedom as one could imagine. Common standards have almost collapsed, and along with them any genuine communication. Characters speak in private idioms and opaque jargon. They collide randomly with one another rather than interrelating. All of this is hilariously prefigured in Laurence Sterne's great eighteenth-century anti-novel *Tristram Shandy*, which is peopled by a bunch of freaks, obsessives, paranoiacs and emotional cripples. This is only one of several reasons why it is among the great comic masterpieces of English literature.

Virtuous literary characters may not be exactly enthralling, but there are novels and plays which seem to be aware of the fact. Fanny Price, the heroine of Jane Austen's *Mansfield Park*, is a dutiful, impeccably well-behaved young woman, and (so many readers of the novel have felt) not a little pallid. She is meek, passive and something of a pain. Yet it is as though the novel has a riposte ready to hand to anyone tactless enough to point this out. How else is a young, unmarried woman without money, social rank or responsible parents to defend herself in the kind of predatory society the novel portrays? Isn't Fanny's lack of vitality an implicit criticism of that social order? She is not, after all, an Emma Woodhouse, rich, attractive, high-ranking and thus able to do pretty well as she likes. Those who are powerful can afford to kick over the traces, whereas the poor and defenceless must look out for themselves. They must court the charge of being insipid in order to avoid graver accusations. If Fanny is something of a drag, it is not her fault. Nor is it the fault of her author, who is well capable of presenting vivacious young women.

One might feel much the same about Charlotte Brontë's Jane Eyre. Self-righteous, moralistic and mildly masochistic, Jane is hardly the most agreeable heroine one could hope to share a taxi with. As a critic once remarked of Samuel Richardson's Pamela, it is not so much that she is scheming as that she is *unconsciously* scheming. Yet it is hard to see how she could be open-hearted and high-spirited in the oppressive circumstances in which she finds herself. As long as there are bigamously minded Rochesters around, as well as religious fanatics like St John Rivers eager to drag you off to an early death in Africa, an orphaned, penniless young woman like Jane would be ill advised to relax her moral vigilance. Pleasantness is for those who can afford it.

This is also true of one of the greatest female figures in English literature, Samuel Richardson's Clarissa. Few characters have received such a mauling at the hands of the critics. Clarissa, who refuses to go to bed with a dissolute aristocrat and is raped by him instead, has been variously described as prudish, priggish, morbid, narcissistic, self-dramatising, masochistic, hypocritical, self-deluded and (this from a female critic) 'a ripe temptation to violence'. Few examples of resplendent virtue have been so cordially detested. Richardson's heroine is certainly pious, high-minded and mildly self-deluded. Yet all she is really doing is protecting her chastity in a brutally patriarchal world. If she is not the kind of woman one would gladly accompany on a pub crawl, unlike Shakespeare's Viola or Thackeray's Becky Sharp, the novel makes it clear enough why she cannot afford to be.

Innocence in a dissolute society is always likely to be mildly amusing. The eighteenth-century novelist Henry Fielding loves his good-hearted characters, like Joseph Andrews and Parson Adams in *Pamela*, but he also delights in sending them up. The innocent are likely to be credulous and naive, and are thus always a rich source of satiric comedy. The good are bound to be gullible, since how can virtue look sharp for itself and still be virtue? To be guileless is as absurd as it is admirable. Fielding thus uses his good-hearted characters to expose the rogues and scoundrels around them, while at the same time poking some gentle fun at their unworldly innocence. If the novel itself were not looking out for their welfare, they would probably sink without trace before the end of the first chapter.

* * *

Some time back, I referred to idiosyncratic characters as 'types', which seems to be something of a contradiction. (The word 'type', incidentally, can also mean a printed letter, just like the word 'character'.) To typecast individuals is to slot them into certain categories rather than to perceive them as beyond compare. Yet it makes perfect sense to speak of a quirky type, not least because there are a lot of them around. Ironically, words like 'quirky', 'oddball' and 'singular' are generic terms, meaning terms referring to a whole group or class. They are quite as generic as 'celibate' or 'courageous'. One can even speak of different types of eccentric. So even freakish people are not unclassifiable. Oddballs can have as much in common with each other as rock climbers or right-wing Republicans.

We like to think of individuals as unique. Yet if this is true of everyone, then we all share the same quality, namely our uniqueness. What we have in common is the fact that we are all uncommon. Everybody is special, which means that nobody is. The truth, however, is that human beings are uncommon only up to a point. There are no qualities that are peculiar to one person alone. Regrettably, there could not be a world in which only one individual was irascible, vindictive or lethally aggressive. This is because human beings are not fundamentally all that different from each other, a truth postmodernists are reluctant to concede. We share an enormous amount in common simply by virtue of being human, and this is revealed by the vocabularies we have for discussing human character. We even share the social processes by which we come to individuate ourselves.

It is true that individuals combine these shared qualities in very different ways, which is part of what makes them so distinctive. But the qualities themselves are common currency. It would make no more sense to claim that only I could be insanely jealous than it would to call the coin in my pocket a dime even though nobody else did. Chaucer and Pope would no doubt have taken this for granted, though Oscar Wilde and Allen Ginsberg would probably have not. Literary critics may think of individuals as incomparable, but sociologists beg to differ. If most human beings were delightfully unpredictable, sociologists would be out of a job. They take no interest in the individual, any more than Stalinists do. Instead, they investigate shared patterns of behaviour. It is a sociological truth that lines at supermarket checkouts are always roughly the same length, since human beings are alike in their reluctance to spend too much time on tedious, relatively trivial tasks such as paying for their groceries. Anyone who queued up just for fun would be seriously strange. It might be a kindness to report him to the social services.

To try to capture the 'essence' of an individual, in the sense of what makes her peculiarly herself, is inevitably to find ourselves using generic terms. This is as true of literature as it is of everyday speech. Literary works are sometimes thought to be concerned above all with the concrete and specific. Yet there is an irony here. A writer may pile phrase upon phrase and adjective upon adjective in order to pin down the elusive essence of a thing. But the more language he throws at a character or situation, the more he tends to bury it beneath a heap of generalities. Or the more he simply buries it beneath language itself. Here, for example, is the celebrated case of Charles Bovary's hat, from Gustave Flaubert's novel *Madame Bovary*:

His was one of those composite pieces of headgear in which you might trace features of bearskin, lancer-cap and bowler, night-cap and otterskin: one of those pathetic objects that are deeply expressive in their dumb ugliness, like an idiot's face. An oval splayed out with whale-bone, it started off with three pompoms; these were followed by lozenges of velvet and rabbit's fur alternately, separated by a red band, and after that came a kind of bag ending in a polygon of cardboard with intricate braiding on it; and from this there hung down like a tassel, at the end of a long, too slender cord, a little sheaf of gold threads. It was a new cap, with a shiny peak.

This is verbal overkill with a vengeance. As critics have pointed out, Charles's cap is almost impossible to visualise. Trying to assemble these details into a coherent whole baffles the imagination. This cap is the kind of object that could exist only in literature. It is a product of language alone. It is impossible to imagine it being worn on the street. By being so absurdly elaborate, Flaubert's description undoes itself. The more a writer specifies, the more information he provides. Yet the more information he provides, the more room he creates for divergent interpretations on the reader's part. And the result of this may not be vividness and specificity but haziness and ambiguity.

In this sense, writing is something of a mug's game. It is as though the Flaubert passage is mischievously making this point, blinding us not with science but with signs. It is a joke at the reader's expense. And what is true of a cap is also true of character. Literary characters, at least in realist fiction, are thought to be at their finest when they are most richly individuated. Yet if they were not also to some extent types, revealing qualities we have encountered before, they would be unintelligible. A completely original literary figure would slip through the net of language, leaving us with nothing whatsoever to say. A type, however, is not necessarily a stereotype. It does not follow from this argument that Aristotle is right when he remarks that it would be inappropriate for an artist to portray a woman as clever. Stereotypes reduce men and women to general categories, whereas types preserve their individuality but lend it some broader context. A cynic might take this to mean that Irishmen are forever engaged in drunken brawling, but that each does so in his own unique way.

It is true that literature, and perhaps poetry above all, can make us feel as though we are in the presence of the irreducibly specific. Yet this involves a certain sleight of hand. Nothing is absolutely specific, if by this one means that it defeats all general categories. We can identify objects only in language, and language is general by nature. If it were not, we would need a different word for every rubber duck and stick of rhubarb in the world. Even terms like 'this', 'here', 'now' and 'utterly unique' are generic. There is no special word for my particular pair of eyebrows or fits of sulkiness. To say 'octopus' is to imply that this specific octopus resembles others. In fact, there is nothing that does not resemble something else in some respect. The Great Wall of China resembles the concept of heartache in that neither can peel a banana.

In any case, the view that literary works deal in the tangible and immediate, rather than the abstract and general, is of fairly recent vintage. It comes to us mostly from the Romantics. Samuel Johnson, writing in the eighteenth century, thought it a lapse of good taste to concern oneself overmuch with the specific. For him, the universal was a good deal more enticing. For some people today, this would be almost as bizarre as finding trigonometry more exciting than sex. This is a sign of how much romanticism, with its passion for the particular, has stealthily transformed our sensibilities.

So nothing is absolutely itself. This, however, is a problem only for post-Romantics. Authors like Dante, Chaucer, Pope and Fielding did not see individuality in quite this way. They did not regard it as the opposite of the general. On the contrary, they recognised that qualities common to the human species went into the making of it. In fact, the word 'individual' used to mean 'indivisible'. It signified that individuals were inseparable from some larger context. Only because we are born into human societies do we become individual persons. This, perhaps, is one reason why the word 'singular' can also mean 'strange'. For the ancients, a monster meant a creature beyond the pale of social existence.

One of the earliest pieces of literary criticism we have, Aristotle's *Poetics*, is mostly a discussion of tragedy, yet its central focus is by no means on character. In fact, Aristotle seems to believe that one could have a tragedy that was entirely without characters. In his play *Breath*, Samuel Beckett goes a few steps further, coming up with a drama that has no plot, characters, storyline, dialogue, scenery or (scarcely) duration. What matters above all for Aristotle is the plot or dramatic action. Individual characters are really just 'supports' for this. They exist not for themselves but for the sake of the action, which Aristotle thinks of as a communal affair. The ancient Greek word for drama literally means 'something done'. Characters may lend the action a certain colouring, but it is what happens that comes first. To overlook this while watching a tragedy would be like treating a football game simply as the acts of a set of solitary individuals, or as a chance for each of them to display 'personality'. The fact that some players behave as though this is precisely what football games are about should not distract us from this point.

It is not that Aristotle thought character unimportant in general. On the contrary, he regarded it as supremely important, as another of his books, the *Nicomachean Ethics*, makes clear. This work is all about moral values, qualities of character, the difference between virtuous and vicious individuals, and so on. Aristotle's view of character in the real-life sense, however, differs from some modern versions of it. Here, too, he sees action as primary. It is what men and women do, the way they realise or fail to realise their creative powers in the public arena, that matters most from a moral view-point. You could not be virtuous simply on your own. Virtue is not like knitting a sock or chewing a carrot. Ancient thinkers were less likely than modern ones to view individuals as existing in splendid isolation. They would no doubt have had some trouble in under-standing Hamlet, not to speak of being utterly bemused by the work of Marcel Proust or Henry James. Being utterly bemused by Proust and James is a familiar experience today as well, but for rather different reasons.

This is not to say that ancient authors regarded men and women as zombies. It is simply that they had rather different notions of consciousness, emotion, psychology and so on from our own. Thinkers like Aristotle are perfectly aware that human beings have an inner life. It is just that they do not typically start from there, as so much Romantic and modernist writing does. Instead, they tend to place this inner life in the context of action, kinship, history and the public world. We have inner lives only because we belong to a language and a culture. We can conceal our thoughts and feelings, of course, but this is a social practice we have to learn. A baby cannot conceal anything. Aristotle also recognised that our public actions have an active influence on our inner lives. Performing virtuous acts helps us to become virtuous. Homer and Virgil begin from men and women as practical, social, embodied beings, and look at human consciousness in this light. So do Aeschylus and Sophocles. The gradual loss of this view of human beings is closely bound up with the withering of our sense of society. Our current notions of literary character are for the most part those of a robustly individualist social order. They are also of quite recent historical origin. They are far from the only way of picturing the human person.

For Aristotle, character is one element in a complex artistic design. It is not to be ripped rudely out of context, as critics used to do when they wrote essays with titles like 'The Girlhood of Ophelia' or 'Would Iago Make a Good Governor of Arizona?' It is true that real-life people are also always encountered in some kind of significant setting. We always perceive each other against some background or other. Human beings are never not in a situation. Not to be sure what situation one is in is to be in the situation known as doubt. To be outside any situation whatsoever is known as being dead. It is true that some people create far more dramatic scenarios by dying than they ever did in living, but these are scenarios for others, not for themselves. Real people, however, since they are more than linguistic creations, have a degree of independence of their surroundings, which is not true of Josef K or the Wife of Bath. Because they can put some daylight between themselves and their situations, they can also transform them, whereas cockroaches and literary characters are stuck with them for ever. The Wife of Bath cannot decide to migrate from *The Canterbury Tales* to *The Sound and the Fury*, whereas we can always kiss goodbye to Sunderland and move to Sacramento.

Because men and women are more than mere functions of their environments, they can come to believe that they are autonomous, a word which literally means 'a law unto oneself'. They can see themselves as standing free of each other and their societies. On this view, they are the source of their own actions, solely and entirely responsible for what they do, ultimately dependent on nothing but themselves. They behave, in short, as Shakespeare describes Coriolanus: 'As if a man were author of himself / And knew no other kin'. It is the assumption that everyone is solely and entirely responsible for what they do that lands so many people on death row in the United States.

This is not a view of human beings that most ancient or medieval thinkers would have endorsed. Neither, one suspects, would Shakespeare. Take, for example, his Othello. Othello is, of course, a character in a play, but he also behaves like one, and tends to regard himself as one. He is full of grandiloquent rhetoric and dramatic self-display. He has the charismatic presence of a man of the theatre. Early in the play's action, he breaks up a fight with the resonant declaration 'Keep up your bright swords, for the dew will rust them.' It is a splendidly attention-grabbing line, as though spoken by an actor playing an actor. Perhaps Othello has been assiduously rehearsing it while waiting in the wings. The words may allude to Jesus' command to his disciples in the Garden of Gethsemane to sheath their swords, which gives them an even more authoritative ring. This man is not only a first-class performer; he even has a touch of the second person of the Blessed Trinity about him. Yet he is, so to speak, an actor of the old school, who regards the stage as a chance to show off his larger-than-life personality, and whose sense of other people is somewhat dim. Teamwork is not Othello's strongest point. He lives straight out of a self-image. It is one of his few points of resemblance to Ernest Hemingway, apart from the fact that Hemingway, too, committed suicide. Othello is a character without a context – literally so, since as a Moor, a man of mixed Berber and Arab stock, he is something of a displaced person in his adopted city of Venice.

The Moor of Venice is a resplendent creation, but we will go astray if we accept his own estimate of himself too readily. There is a histrionic quality to this hero. He is a man who seems curiously aware that he is speaking Shakespearian blank verse:

> Never, Iago. Like to the Pontic sea,
> Whose icy current and compulsive course
> Ne'er feels retiring ebb, but keeps due on
> To the Propontic and the Hellespont;
> Even so my bloody thoughts, with violent pace,
> Shall ne'er look back, ne'er ebb to humble love,
> Till that a capable and wide revenge
> Swallow them up . . .

Othello dies at the end of the play, as tragic heroes tend to do, but he is determined to go out on a high theatrical note:

> Set you down this:
> And say besides that in Aleppo once,
> Where a malignant and a turban'd Turk
> Beat a Venetian and traduc'd the state,
> I took by th' throat the circumcised dog,
> And smote him – thus. (**He stabs himself**)

As one critic wryly comments, it is a magnificent *coup de théâtre*. This man can even turn the act of stabbing himself into a self-congratulatory gesture. He idealises himself even at the point of death.

By setting Othello in the context of the play as a whole, seeing how its mode of characterising him is interwoven with theme, plot, mood, imagery and so on, we can come up with an idea of literary character rather different from his own. He no longer appears such a grandly autonomous being. This is one way to avoid speaking of characters as though they lived in your apartment building. Hamlet is not simply a despondent young prince; he is also an occasion for certain reflections by the play as a whole, the embodiment of certain ways of seeing and modes of feeling which stretch far beyond himself. He is a complex of insights and preoccupations rather than just a student with a shady stepfather. We also need to examine the techniques by which character is manufactured. Is a particular literary figure presented simply as a type or emblem, or is she subtly psychologised? Is she grasped from the inside or treated from other characters' standpoints? Is she seen as coherent or self-contradictory, static or evolving, firmly etched or fuzzy at the edges? Are characters viewed in the round or stripped to functions of the plot? Are they defined through their actions and relationships, or do they loom up as disembodied consciousnesses? Do we feel them as vivid physical presences or essentially verbal ones, as readily knowable or as full of elusive depths?

One of the achievements of the great European realist novel, from Stendhal and Balzac to Tolstoy and Thomas Mann, is to illustrate this interweaving of character and context. Characters in this kind of fiction are seen as caught up in a web of complex mutual dependencies. They are formed by social and historical forces greater than themselves, and shaped by processes of which they may be only fitfully conscious. This is not to say that they are just the playthings of these powers. On the contrary, they play an active part in shaping their own destinies. But it is not as though the whole of reality is spun out of the guts of a few great men existing in splendid isolation. As George Eliot puts it, there is no private life that has not been influenced by a wider public one. The realist novel tends to grasp individual lives in terms of histories, communities, kinship and institutions. It is in these frameworks that the self is seen as embedded. Just as there are many things that go into the making of a literary work beside an author, so there are many things that go into the making of a realist character. There is a difference between this realist project and the modernist novel, which quite often presents us with a single, solitary consciousness. Think, for example, of Beckett's *Malone Dies* or Woolf's *Mrs Dalloway*.

Characters in the realist tradition are generally presented as complex, credible, fully rounded individuals. Many of them seem a lot more real than the people next door. Some of them are also a lot more agreeable. Without this array of superbly realised figures, some of whom have assumed the status of myth and legend, world literature would be much the poorer. Even so, we should be aware that the realist idea of character is only one of several. There are many works of literature which are not especially eager to tell us what the protagonist had for breakfast, or what colour of socks his chauffeur wears. The New Testament represents Jesus as a character of sorts, but it has no interest in delving into his mind. Such psychologising would be irrelevant to its purposes. The work is not intended to be a biography. It does not even tell us what its central character looked like. If they were taking a creative writing course today, the Gospel writers might well find themselves handed a shamefully low grade.

The same relative indifference to what goes on inside people's heads can be found in the Book of Isaiah, Dante's *Divine Comedy*, the medieval mystery plays, Jonathan Swift's *Gulliver's Travels*, Daniel Defoe's *Moll Flanders*, Bertolt Brecht's *The Threepenny Opera* and a good many other eminent works of literature. One of the finest of twentieth-century English authors, Evelyn Waugh, once observed that 'I regard writing not as an investigation of character, but as an exercise in the use of language, and with this I am obsessed. I have no technical psychological interest. It is drama, speech and events that interest me.' Aristotle would have understood what he meant, though Scott Fitzgerald might have been somewhat mystified.

The modernists are in search of new modes of characterisation, suitable to a post-Victorian age. What it feels like to be a person is not quite the same for Franz Kafka as it is for George Eliot, and certainly not for whoever wrote the Upanishads or the Book of Daniel. Eliot sees character as 'a process and an unfolding', which is not at all how Woolf or Beckett regard it. For them, human beings do not have that much consistency and continuity. The typical realist character tends to be reasonably stable and unified, more like Amy Dorrit or David Copperfield than Joyce's Stephen Dedalus or T.S. Eliot's Gerontion. As such, it reflects an era when identity was felt on the whole to be less problematic than it is today. People could still see themselves as the agents of their own destinies. They had a fairly acute sense of where they stopped and other people began. Their personal and collective history, for all its ups and downs, seems to represent a coherent evolution, one which was more likely to issue in felicity than in catastrophe.

Modernism, by contrast, pitches the whole concept of identity into crisis. Stephen Dedalus and Leopold Bloom, the twin protagonists of James Joyce's *Ulysses*, appear to be in reasonable command of their lives as they stroll aimlessly around Dublin. This, however, is a kind of joke at their expense, since the reader is conscious that a good deal of what they do is determined by the novel's Homeric subplot. They themselves are not aware that their lives are being secretly scripted in this way, since they are not readers of the novel in which they appear. It is as though they stand to the Homeric subplot as the ego stands to the unconscious. We shall see later that modernism also throws orthodox notions of narrative into question, in a world where it is becoming hard to deliver an agreed, coherent, overarching account of human affairs. In *Ulysses*, for example, very little happens. Or at least, as with the Marabar Caves, it is hard to say whether anything happens or not. In *Waiting for Godot*, as one critic famously remarked, nothing happens twice over, first in Act 1 and then in Act 2.

So the modernists seek to question stock notions of character. Some of them do so by pressing the psychological complexity of literary figures to the point where character in its classical sense begins to disintegrate. Once you start to see human consciousness as unfathomably intricate, it is hard to contain it within the well-defined limits of Walter Scott's Rob Roy or Robert Louis Stevenson's Jim Hawkins. Instead, it begins to spill out over the edges, seeping into its surroundings as well as into other selves. This is especially true of Virginia Woolf's fiction, where identity is more elusive and indeterminate than it is in Trollope or Thomas Hardy. This indeterminacy is not always to be applauded, as postmodernists tend to assume. It can involve a traumatic sense of loss and anxiety. Having too little identity can be quite as disabling as having too much.

If the self is bound up with its changing experiences, then it no longer has the unity and consistency of Bunyan's Everyman or Shakespeare's Coriolanus. It is less able to recount a coherent story of itself. Its beliefs and desires do not necessarily hang together to form a seamless whole. Neither do the works in which such characters appear. From Aristotle to the present day, critics have tended to assume that literary works should be tightly integrated wholes, with not a stray symbol dangling or a hair out of place. But why should this necessarily be a value? Can't conflict and dissonance be commendable as well? Perhaps, as Woolf sometimes suspects, the self is just a bundle of chance sensations and perceptions, with only a vacancy at its core. Joyce's Leopold Bloom has a modernist mind of this kind, responsive to fragments of sensation but with little continuity. It is true that he is also a fully rounded, painstakingly detailed figure, but this is among other things a satirical send-up of the realist or naturalistic notion of character. If George Eliot shows her characters seated at breakfast, Joyce will go one step further and show its hero seated on the lavatory. Bloom is the creation of a dissident Irishman taking a smack at the stoutly realist British. Oscar Wilde, another subversive Irishman who made a career out of baiting the British, described truth as 'one's latest mood'. For him to be truly free meant to be free of a consistent selfhood, as well as being free to bed the sons of the English nobility.

There is another way in which modernist works seek to dismantle traditional ideas of character. This is by trying to reveal something of the forces that shape the self at the deepest level. D.H. Lawrence declared that he was not concerned with character or personality, since the depths of selfhood he was plumbing lay far beneath the conscious ego. In the wake of Freud, orthodox notions of identity are bound to be thrown into question. Conscious life is now just the tip of the iceberg of the self. The selfhood which Lawrence explores lies somewhere on the far side of ideas, emotions, personality, moral viewpoints or routine relationships. It belongs to some dark, primeval, profoundly impersonal realm of being. And this is a terrain where realist authors could not hope to tread. The self for Lawrence is not something we can master. It has its own enigmatic logic, and will go its own sweet way. We are really strangers to ourselves. And if we are not in possession of ourselves, then we cannot foist our identities on others either. So there is an ethics and a politics involved in this way of seeing.

T.S. Eliot is also disdainful of mere consciousness, and largely indifferent to individual personality. What seizes his attention are the myths and traditions which shape the individual self. It is these deeper forces that his work seeks to elicit. And these forces lie far below the individual mind, in a kind of collective unconscious. It is here that we all share in the same timeless myths and spiritual wisdom. So the conscious meaning of a poem does not matter all that much. This is why Eliot did not greatly care what interpretations of his work readers came up with. It is the impact his poetry makes on the guts, the nervous system and the unconscious which concerns him most. It is ironic, then, that Eliot is often seen as a dauntingly intellectual author. His poetry is full of cryptic symbolism and erudite allusions. Yet 'intellectual' is one of the last words to describe his writing. His poems are built out of words, images and sensations rather than ideas. In fact, he did not believe that a poet could think in his poetry at all.

True to this anti-intellectualism, Eliot once remarked that his ideal reader would be an uneducated one. He himself claimed to enjoy Dante in the original without being able to read Italian. Fool that you are, you might think you haven't a clue what is going on in *The Waste*

*Land* and *Four Quartets*, but at some subliminal level you are under-standing them all the time. Among other things, this is because those lucky enough to live in Europe are part of something called the European Mind, whether they know it or not. But an Indonesian fisherman could probably grasp the meaning of *The Waste Land* too, since he has intuitive knowledge of the great spiritual archetypes on which it draws. It might help if he was also able to read English, though perhaps it is not essential. That one can understand *The Waste Land* without even trying is consoling news for all students of literature. Perhaps the same is true of the General Theory of Relativity. Maybe we are all nuclear physicists somewhere deep in our guts.

There is another reason why the idea of character as Balzac or Hawthorne knew it no longer seems feasible in modern times. This is because in an age of mass culture and commerce, human beings come to seem increasingly faceless and interchangeable. We can distinguish easily enough between Othello and Iago, but not between Beckett's Vladimir and Estragon. The characters of *The Waste Land*, as Eliot himself remarked, are not really distinct from one another. Leopold Bloom, as we have seen, is sharply individu-alised, yet he is also an anonymous Everyman whose thoughts and feelings could be almost anybody's. His mind is magnificently banal. Figures in Virginia Woolf tend to blur into each other, as feelings and sensations pass like vibrations from one individual to the next. It is becoming harder to identify the owner of a particular experience. Joyce's *Finnegans Wake* contains characters of a sort, but like figures in a dream they seem perpetually to merge, split, dissolve and recombine, secreting within themselves a whole array of fractured selves and provisional identities. One might say of a good deal of modernist writing that the true protagonist is not this or that character, but language itself.

\* \* \*

We may now look at a particular literary character in rather more detail. Sue Bridehead of Thomas Hardy's *Jude the Obscure* ranks among the most stunningly original portraits of a woman in Victorian fiction. Yet the novel lays a trap for the unwary reader. It is as though it deliberately tempts him to write Sue off as perverse, flirtatious and exasperatingly fickle, and many a reader has obediently fallen for the bait. As one sternly judgemental critic of Sue writes,

> there isn't, when one comes down to it, much to be said in her defence. Having speeded on the death of her first lover, Sue captivates Jude to enjoy the thrill of being loved, and then enters with dubious motives and curiously mechanical detachment into marriage with Phillotson, treating Jude with astounding callousness in the process. Having refused to sleep with Phillotson she abandons him for Jude, temporarily wrecking the schoolmaster's career, and refuses to sleep with Jude too. She then agrees to marry him out of jealousy of Arabella, changes her mind, and finally returns again to Phillotson, leaving Jude to die ... The problem is how we come to feel that Sue is more than just a perverse hussy, full of petty stratagems and provocative pouts; for that this is at one level an accurate description of her seems undeniable.

It may have seemed undeniable to me when I wrote these words some forty years ago in the Preface to the New Wessex edition of the novel, but they strike me today as woefully off the mark. Sue is not full of provocative pouts. She pouts once in the novel, unprovocatively. Neither is she a schemer, as the phrase 'full of petty stratagems' would suggest. It is not at all clear that she 'speeded on' the death of her first lover. He claims that she broke his heart, but the charge is pretty preposterous. Not many people die of this particular ailment, not least when they are gravely ill in any case, as Sue's first lover seems to have been. Nor does she treat Jude with 'astounding callousness'. It is not her fault that Phillotson is hounded out of his job. The passage is a tissue of untruths. If Sue were alive today, she could sue for defamation of character. She could, however, screw a lot more damages out of D.H. Lawrence, who brands her in his *Study of Thomas Hardy* as 'almost male', 'an 'old-woman type of witch' who adheres to the 'male principle' and is 'scarcely a woman at all'. Rather oddly, Lawrence also accuses her of being 'physically impotent'. So Sue is really a man, but a man who is not a real man. It is hard to get more sexually confused than that.

It is true (to do my younger self a spot of justice) that I proposed this version of Sue as only one possible reading. It is also true that she can be jealous, capricious and exasperatingly inconsistent. These, however, are hardly hanging offences. Much of Sue's behaviour makes sense once one sees that it is driven by a deep fear of sexuality. This is not because she is a Victorian prude, but for exactly the opposite reason. She is an enlightened young woman with boldly progressive views about marriage and sexuality. She is also something of a sceptic when it comes to religious belief. The irony is that she is wary of sexuality precisely because of her emancipated views. She regards marriage and sexuality as snares which rob women of their independence, and the novel itself fully supports her in this opinion. ' "Is it," [Jude] said, "that the women are to blame; or is it the artificial system of things, under which the normal sex-impulses are turned into devilish domestic gins and springes [that is, traps] to noose and hold back those who want to progress?" ' (Whether anyone ever spoke like this in real life is another question.) If she tries to disavow her love for Jude, with calamitous consequences for them both, it is not because she is heartless but because she recognises that love in these social conditions is inseparable from oppressive power. Sexuality is about subjugation. As Hardy writes in *Far from the Madding Crowd*, 'it is difficult for a woman to define her feelings in language which is chiefly made by men to express theirs'.

If Sue finds it hard to commit herself to Jude, it is not because she is a flirt but because she values her freedom. She grew up, so we are told, as something of a tomboy; and this epicene or sexless quality, which puts her beyond the pale of conventional sexual behaviour, makes it hard for her to understand men's sexual feelings for her. She can thus hurt them without intending to. She would prefer simply to be their friends. The novel sees with extraordinary insight that the sexual institutions of late Victorian society have destroyed the possibility of comradeship between men and women. Some of Sue's apparent perversity springs from the fact that her advanced sexual views are inevitably somewhat theoretical. Women's emancipation is still at an early stage. So her beliefs can easily succumb to social pressures. She is thrown out of college for unbecoming conduct, and then, alarmed by the public outcry this occasions, tries to set matters right with respectable opinion by marrying the mildly repulsive Phillotson. The result is predictably disastrous.

Throughout the book, Sue has a dismally low estimate of herself. She is a far more admirable woman than she imagines, and the novel allows us to see the discrepancy between what she is really like and her own self-loathing. When an adopted child of Jude and Sue hangs their other children and then kills himself, an event which the novel does not even try to make realistically convincing, Sue's poor opinion of herself is pressed to a pathological extreme. 'I should like to prick myself all over with pins,' she cries, 'and bleed out the badness that's in me!' Convulsed by guilt and self-disgust, she abandons Jude and returns to Phillotson, leaving Jude to die wretched and alone. I note this fact in my Preface, but fail to mention that Sue leaves her partner for the most understandable of reasons. It is hardly surprising that a woman who has just lost her children in this grotesque manner, and who is in any case the target of vicious public censure, should take the death of her children as divine punishment for her bohemian way of life, and finally submit to moral orthodoxy. It is understandable not least because Sue's sexual emancipation is still embryonic and uncertain. It is a work in progress rather than an achieved position. How could it be otherwise when she is forced to go it alone, with no support from society at large and a good deal of prejudice and hostility to face down?

The tragedy of the novel is that Sue and Jude try to live out a form of comradeship, but are thwarted in the end by the power of patriarchy. Even a love as deep and steadfast as theirs is bent out of true by the system. 'Sexuality is blood-stained,' as one commentator on the book remarks. This superbly courageous novel is about the impossibility of sexuality, not just its pitfalls and illusions. Yet it refuses to accept that the couple's failure was somehow fated. It has nothing to do with Nature, Providence or a malevolent God. It is just that the experiment was premature. History was not yet ready for it. The same is true of Jude's ill-starred attempt to enter Oxford University as a working man. This project, too, was not doomed but before its time, as he himself comes to acknowledge. Not long after his death, a college for working people was established in Oxford, and still exists today. In any case, the novel suggests with cold-eyed realism that for its hero to try to break into the benighted set-up known as Oxford University was not worth the effort. Repairing the walls of the very colleges which shut him out, which is one of Jude's jobs, is more useful in Hardy's eyes than most of the learning that goes on within them.

One reason why it is easy for critics to see Sue as frigid and neurotic is that we view her largely through the eyes of others. We are not allowed much access to her from the inside. For much of the narrative, she exists as a function of Jude's experience, not as a character in her own right. If she seems so tantalisingly opaque, it is partly because she is filtered through the needs, desires and delusions of the protagonist. As one critic puts it, she is made the instrument of Jude's tragedy rather than the subject of her own. It is not surprising that after Jude's death she is no longer seen at all. To this extent, the novel itself is complicit in the sidelining of its heroine. But it is also extraordinarily perceptive in its presentation of her.

\* \* \*

*Jude the Obscure* invites us to sympathise with Sue Bridehead, but it also wants us to see how she escapes any simple understanding. If nobody in the novel itself can truly own her, the same is true of its readers. We are asked to feel for Sue, but not in a way that irons out her inconsistencies. Some of the book's other characters, including from time to time Jude himself, mistake her elusiveness for the eternal enigma of Woman. On the whole, however, the novel itself refuses this patronising viewpoint. Sue's 'mystery' springs largely from the complex, self-contradictory nature of sexuality in a social order which puts it to oppressive uses.

A good deal of realist fiction invites the reader to identify with its characters. We are supposed to feel what it is like to be someone else, even if we would not relish the thought of actually being them. By allowing us imaginatively to recreate the experience of other human beings, the realist novel broadens and deepens our human sympathies. In this sense, it is a moral phenomenon without actually having to moralise. It is moral, if you like, by virtue of its form, not just its content. George Eliot is a writer who does indeed moralise rather too much for modern taste, but she herself saw the novel form in just this light. 'The only effect I ardently long to produce by my writings,' she writes in a letter, 'is that those who read them should be better able to *imagine* and to *feel* the pains and joys of those who differ from themselves in everything but the broad fact of being struggling erring human creatures.' For Eliot, the creative imagination is the opposite of egoism. It allows us to enter into the inner lives of others, rather than remaining sealed off from them in our own private spheres. The artistic is thus very close to the ethical. If only we could grasp the world from someone else's standpoint, we would have a fuller sense of how and why they act as they do. We would thus be less inclined to reproach them from some loftily external point of view. To understand is to forgive.

This charitable case has much to recommend it. But there is quite a lot wrong with it as well. For one thing, not all literary art invites us to identify with its characters. For another thing, empathy is not the only form of understanding. In fact, taken literally, it is not a form of understanding at all. If I 'become' you, I lose my faculty of knowing what you are like. Who is left over to do the understanding? Besides, are we supposed to empathise with nasty pieces of work like Dracula, or Mrs Norris in *Mansfield Park*? (There may be a few seriously bizarre people who would like nothing better than to be a vampire, but most of us would prefer to be Odysseus or Elizabeth Bennet.) Anyway, if I 'become' Hector or Homer Simpson, I can understand them only if they understand themselves, which seems far from true in Homer's case. D.H. Lawrence is especially sardonic about empathy in his *Studies in American Literature*. 'As soon as Walt [Whitman] *knew* a thing,' he writes, 'he assumed a One Identity with it. If he knew that an Eskimo sat in a kyak, immediately there was Walt being little and yellow and greasy, sitting in a kyak'. The critical point survives the casual racism.

Sophocles is not inviting us to empathise with Oedipus. The play expects us to feel pity for its doomed protagonist, but there is a difference between feeling for someone (sympathy) and feeling as them (empathy). If we merge ourselves imaginatively with Oedipus, how can we pass judgement on him? Yet this is surely an important part of what criticism involves. To judge involves holding something a little at arm's length, a move which is compatible with sympathy but not with empathy. The literary art of ancient Greece does not ask us to feel what it is like to have a spear through one's guts or a monster in one's womb. Instead, it puts characters and events on display for our appraisal. So does a neo-classical author like Henry Fielding. We are expected to observe Tom Jones with an amused, ironic, sympathetic eye, not climb into bed with him. There are quite enough people in bed with him already.

The Marxist dramatist Bertolt Brecht, writing in the age of Hitler, thought that empathising with characters on stage risked blunting our critical faculties. And this, he considered, was highly convenient for those in power. Empathy elevated sentiment over critical reason. As a Marxist, Brecht also believed that social existence was made up of contradictions, and that these contradictions went to the heart of people's identities. To show men and women as they really are is to show them as changeable, inconsistent and self-divided. The idea of character as unified and coherent struck Brecht as an illusion. It repressed the conflicts within the self which might make for social change. In one of his short stories, Herr Keuner, who has been absent from his village for many years, returns home, and is cheerfully informed by his neighbours that he hasn't changed a bit. 'Herr Keuner,' Brecht writes, 'turned white.' Behind Scott or Balzac's conception of character lies one kind of politics; behind Brecht's lies another. He was the only man in history who was banned from the Danish communist party before he had applied to join.

If imaginative sympathy is only one way of approaching character, it also has some more general limitations. The phrase 'the creative imagination' is one which almost everyone on the planet seems to find unequivocally positive, like 'We're off to Marrakesh tomorrow' or 'Have another Guinness'. But the imagination is by no means unambiguously positive. Serial killing requires a fair amount of imagination. The imagination is able to project all kinds of dark, diseased scenarios as well as a great many affirmative ones. Every lethal weapon ever invented was the result of an act of imagination. The imagination is thought to be among the noblest of human faculties, but it is also unnervingly akin to fantasy, which is generally ranked among the lowest.

In any case, trying to feel what you are feeling will not necessarily improve my moral character. A sadist likes to know what his victim is feeling. Someone may need to know how you are feeling in order to exploit you more effectively. The Nazis did not kill Jews because they could not identify with what they were feeling. They did not care what they were feeling. I cannot experience the pains of childbirth, but this does not mean that I am callously indifferent to someone who does. Morality has precious little to do with feeling in any case. The fact that you feel a surge of nausea at the sight of someone with half their head shot away is neither here nor there as long as you try to help them. Conversely, feeling intense compassion for someone who has just fallen down a manhole, while nipping down a side-street to avoid having to haul him out, will not win you many humanitarian prizes.

Literature is sometimes thought of as a 'vicarious' mode of experience. I cannot know what it feels like to be a skunk, but a gripping short story with a skunk at its centre might allow me to overcome my restrictions in this respect. But there is no particular value in knowing what it feels like to be a skunk. Acts of imagination are not precious in themselves. It is not testimony to my sublime creativity that I spend most of the day trying to imagine what it would feel like to be a vacuum cleaner. It does not feel like anything to be a vacuum cleaner. Nor is the imaginary always to be preferred to the real. To suppose that it should be, as some Romantics do, implies a curiously negative attitude to everyday reality. It suggests that what does not exist is always more glamorous or alluring than what does. This may be true if you are thinking of Donald Trump, but not if you are thinking of Nelson Mandela.

There is no doubt that we can usefully extend our experience by reading works of literature. It is just that this can also be a way of compensating for deficiencies that might be set right for real. Those with enough money and leisure, for example, can explore the mountainous region between Pakistan and Afghanistan. Most people on the planet lack the resources to enjoy this experience, and are reluctant to join al-Qa'ida in order to have it for free. They must settle for reading travel books instead. If wealth were shared more equally, however, a lot more people might be able to swarm over the area, provided they were willing to risk getting shot. One advantage of reading a Lonely Planet guidebook on the place is that nobody is likely to plug you with a bullet for doing so. In the nineteenth century, literature was sometimes recommended to the working classes as a way of feeling what it was like to ride to hounds or marry a viscount, since they were not able to do these things in reality. There have been more persuasive arguments for why poems and novels are worth reading.

# CHAPTER 3

# Narrative

Some narrators in fiction are known as omniscient, meaning that they are assumed to know everything about the story they tell and that the reader is not expected to question what they say. If a novel begins 'Stately, plump Buck Mulligan came from the stairhead, bearing a bowl of lather on which a mirror and a razor lay crossed,' it would be futile for the reader to exclaim, 'No, he didn't!', 'How do you know?' or 'Don't give me that!' The fact that we have just read the words 'A Novel' on the title page rules out these questions as invalid. We are supposed to bow to the authority of the narrator. If he tells us that Mulligan was carrying a bowl of lather, then we obediently collude in the illusion that he was, rather as we collude in the illusion that a toddler is the President of the International Monetary Fund if this yields him some momentary pleasure.

Bowing to the narrator's authority, however, is not much of a risk, since we are not signing on for very much. We are not really being asked to believe that there was someone called Buck Mulligan who carried a bowl of lather. It would be truer to say that we are being asked to make-believe it. We know from reading the words 'A Novel', or simply from knowing that this text is intended as fiction, that the author is not trying to fool us into imagining that this actually took place. He is not offering the statement as a proposition about the real world. It is said that an eighteenth-century bishop who read Jonathan Swift's novel *Gulliver's Travels* threw the book into the fire, indignantly declaring that he didn't believe a word of it. He obviously thought that the story was meant to be true, but suspected that it was invented. Which, of course, is just what it is. The bishop was dismissing the fiction because he thought it was fiction.

If the statement about Mulligan is not meant to fool us, it can be claimed rather oddly that it is neither true nor false. This is because only assertions about reality can be true or false, and this sentence does not count as one of them. It just looks as though it does. It has the form of one, but not the content. So we are not expected to believe it, but neither are we expected to shout, 'Come off it!' or 'What a load of nonsense!' To do so would be to imply that the author intended to make a genuine claim about the world, which is clearly not the case. In the same way, 'Good morning' sounds like a proposition about reality ('It's a good morning'), but is in fact the expression of a wish ('I trust you have a good morning'). And this cannot be true or false, any more than 'Give me a break!', 'Who are you staring at?' or 'You disgusting little two-timer' can be. It is not true that there was a murderous Russian student called Raskolnikov or a down-at-heel salesman named Willy Loman. However, to say so in a work of literature is not false either, since the work is not claiming that there was.

Omniscient narrators are disembodied voices rather than locatable characters. In their anonymous, unidentifiable fashion, they act as the mind of the work itself. Even so, we should not assume that they express a real-life author's thoughts and sentiments. We have seen an example of this already in the opening lines of

E.M. Forster's *A Passage to India*, which are spoken by an omniscient narrator but which register attitudes that may or may not be Forster's own. The town of Chandrapore does not exist, so Forster cannot have any opinions about it. He can hold views about India in general, but what he writes in this passage may be as much for literary effect as a reflection of them. There is rarely any simple relation between authors and their works. Sean O'Casey's play *The Plough and the Stars* pokes merciless fun at a character called the Covey, who spouts Marxist jargon and insists that the workers' struggle must take precedence over national liberation. Yet O'Casey was himself a Marxist, and believed precisely what the Covey preaches. Joyce's *A Portrait of the Artist as a Young Man* concludes with its hero producing a long, erudite argument about aesthetics, some of which we can be fairly sure Joyce himself did not accept. But the novel does not tell us so.

There are times when who exactly is doing the narrating in a piece of fiction is not entirely clear. Take, for example, this passage from Saul Bellow's novel *Henderson the Rain King*:

> Daylight came from a narrow opening above my head; this light was originally yellow but became gray by contact with stones. In the opening two iron spikes were set to keep even a child from creeping through. Examining my situation I found a small passage cut from the granite which led downward to another flight of stairs, which were of stone too. These were narrower and ran to a greater depth, and soon I found them broken, with grass springing and soil leaking out through the cracks. 'King', I called, 'King, hey, are you down there, Your Highness?' But nothing came from below except drafts of warm air that lifted up the spider webs. 'What's the guy's hurry?', I thought . . .

The passage is supposedly spoken by Henderson, the book's hero. Yet Henderson is a rough-and-ready American who might well exclaim 'King, hey' or 'What's the guy's hurry?', but would hardly speak in poetic vein of the yellow light becoming grey by contact with the stones. Nor is he likely to write prose as relatively formal as 'Examining my situation I found a small passage cut from the granite . . .' This is a hybrid narration, in which Henderson's own voice is woven into the more sophisticated tones of the author himself. The novel's linguistic scope would be too limited if it could not reach beyond the consciousness of its main character. Yet it needs to let his own style of speaking come through as well.

I have said that omniscient narrators are assumed to know every-thing there is to know about their stories, but there are occasional exceptions to this rule. A narrator, for example, may feign ignorance of something in his tale. In a mediocre detective story entitled *The Footsteps at the Lock*, one of the characters lights up a cheap ciga-rette, and the rather snobbish author pretends not to know what brand it is. I say 'pretends', but it is not as though he really knows but is concealing the fact. If the reader is not told the brand, there isn't one. We have here a species of that rare phenomenon, a brand-less cigarette (I leave aside the knotty question of roll-ups). You can have cigarettes of this kind in literature, just as you can have a grin without a cat, an Albanian-speaking ostrich or someone who is simultaneously drinking whisky in Birmingham, England and performing brain surgery in Birmingham, Alabama. Real life is less pleasantly diverse in this respect. As Oscar Wilde remarked, art is a place where one thing can be true, but also its opposite. It is more economical than everyday life. One thinks of the final sentences of Samuel Beckett's novel *Molloy*: 'It is midnight. The rain is beating on the window. It was not midnight. It was not raining.'

There are unreliable narrators as well as omniscient ones. The governess who narrates Henry James's *The Turn of the Screw* is almost certainly insane. James is playing a devious game with the reader, providing us with enough grounds to credit the governess's account while dropping sufficient sly hints to suggest that it is not to be trusted. We have seen already that Nelly Dean's narrative in *Wuthering Heights* is not entirely dependable. Jane Eyre delivers a tale tinged with pride, resentment, envy, anxiety, aggression and self-interest. Some of Joseph Conrad's narrators draw attention to the limited nature of their own powers of interpretation. They may have only a fitful, confused sense of what is going on in the stories they tell. The narrator of Conrad's *Under Western Eyes* is a case in point, as are the storytellers of Ford Madox Ford's *The Good Soldier* and Thomas Mann's *Doctor Faustus*. It is possible that such narrators grasp less of the significance of the story than the reader does herself. We can see what they cannot see, and perhaps why they cannot see it.

A notoriously unreliable storyteller is the hero of Jonathan Swift's *Gulliver's Travels*. Gulliver, who never seems to learn anything from his travels, is a boneheaded narrator as well as an unreliable one. All boneheaded narrators are unreliable, but not all unreliable narrators are boneheaded. Gulliver acts as the focus of the book's satire, but in a neat double-tactic he is also the target of it. He can be pathetically keen to identify with the outlandish creatures he finds himself among. In Lilliput, for example, he takes on the standards of this nation of tiny creatures far too eagerly. At one point, he hotly denies the charge of having had sex with a female Lilliputan who is only a few inches high. He also fails to raise the obvious impossibility of this in his own defence. He is also foolishly proud of the title these midgets bestow on him. Gulliver, in short, is something of a gull.

Swift himself was Anglo-Irish, and as such felt fully at home in neither Ireland nor Britain. One way to resolve this dilemma, as Oscar Wilde was to discover, is to become more English than the English themselves, a strategy reflected in Gulliver's obsequious behaviour. By the close of the novel, having lived for a while with the horse-like Houyhnhnms, he is trotting around the place whinnying. Not many narrators are shown going off their heads within their own narratives. At other times, however, Gulliver is too out of touch with local customs, as a chuckleheaded Englishman complacently blind to his own cultural prejudices. He is always either too far out, or in over his head. Swift uses his narrator to expose the cruelty and corruption of others, but also heaps ridicule on him within his own tale.

If you tell your story from the standpoint of a specific character, it may not be easy to step outside this perspective. A literary work written from the viewpoint of a frog risks imprisoning itself in a froglike world. It is hard for it to rise above the consciousness of its own narrator. Not many narrators are frogs, but quite a few are children. This may have its charms, as with the much loved teenage narrator of *The Catcher in the Rye*, but it can also have its drawbacks. To see the world from a child's viewpoint can make it seem revealingly unfamiliar. It may be to perceive objects with a peculiar freshness and immediacy, as Wordsworth is aware. Yet a child's way of seeing is naturally restricted. (A notable exception to this rule is Maisie Farange of Henry James's novel *What Maisie Knew*, a little girl who seems to be almost as omniscient as her author.) Dickens's David Copperfield tells us that as a boy he was able to see in pieces, but not in the round. Ironically, this is the way Dickens himself tends to perceive. A child's vision of reality may be vivid but fragmentary, and so, often enough, is Dickens's own way of looking.

There is thus something peculiarly appropriate about the fact that he so often gazes at the world through the eyes of a child.

The limited vision of child narrators means that they cannot always make coherent sense of their experience. This can lead to some amusing or alarming situations. But it also means that a character like Oliver Twist can have no understanding of the system under which he suffers. All he wants is some immediate help, an impulse with which we naturally sympathise. Yet without some sense of how the system works, and how to change it, there will be many more children gazing up past Mr Bumble's ample belly in search of extra gruel. In this early novel, Dickens himself seems unable to grasp that there is more at issue here than the cruelty of individuals or the question of raw need. What is at stake is the heartless logic of a whole society, as the later Dickens would come to recognise. We shall be investigating this later in the case of *Great Expectations*.

Some narrators are unreliable to the point of being outright cheats. The narrator of Agatha Christie's detective thriller *The Murder of Roger Ackroyd* is actually the murderer, but the authority with which he is invested by the act of telling the story throws us off the scent. The murderer in a detective story is usually hidden, but hidden by the plot, not concealed behind the act of narrating. We learn at the end of Flann O'Brien's *The Third Policeman* that the narrator has been dead for most of the novel, just as we are shocked to discover at the end of William Golding's novel *Pincher Martin* that Martin, who tells the story, was drowned on the first page.

The speaker of Andrew Marvell's poem 'To His Coy Mistress', a man apparently haunted by the fear of death, urges his mistress to overcome her maidenly modesty and make love to him before they both land up in the grave. He is not exactly an unreliable narrator, but it is certainly prudent for both mistress and reader to mistrust his motives. Is he really distraught by the brevity of life and love, or is he just trying to get her to sleep with him? Is this the most intellectual attempt to bed a woman on human record? Is the speaker in earnest in his musings about mortality, or is this simply an artful device to persuade his mistress that she might as well indulge the pleasures of the flesh while she still has some flesh to indulge? The poem does not allow us to choose between these alternatives. Instead, it allows them to co-exist in a kind of ironic tension, playful and pressing at the same time. Maybe the narrator himself has no idea of how serious he is intending to be.

There has been some argument among critics over whether Thady Quirk, the narrator of Maria Edgeworth's novel *Castle Rackrent*, is an unreliable narrator or not. Thady is a servant of the Irish aristocratic Rackrent family, and to all outward appearances a faithful old retainer. He recounts the history of his drunken, black-hearted employers with obsequious affection. Throughout the book, he displays a genial indulgence of the vices of his superiors, which include such endearing little foibles as Sir Kit Rackrent imprisoning his wife in her bedroom for seven years. One can thus read the novel as a satire of the way servants can be conned into complicity with their masters, a complicity which is more in their masters' interests than their own. In this sense, the novel is a fable of misplaced loyalties.

Yet this is not the only reading possible. We can also see Thady as a type of the rebellious Irish peasantry, craftily concealing his disaffection beneath a mask of servility. Perhaps he is secretly working for the overthrow of the landlords, and thus seeking to promote the old Gaelic dream of the common people reclaiming the land. There are clues in the novel to suggest such a scheme.

Thady commits a number of self-serving blunders and oversights which might well be more intentional than they seem. By the end of the story, his son Jason has managed to lay his hands on the Rackrent estates, perhaps with his father's secret connivance. In which case Thady is fooling not only his masters but the reader as well, who is never for a moment allowed into his confidence. Seen from this angle, he is a stereotype of the cringing, duplicitous Irish peasantry, who swear loyalty to their landowner during the day while creeping out to hamstring his cattle at night. On yet another reading, however, Thady is fooling himself rather than the reader. In a classic act of self-deception, he believes he is faithful to the Rackrents but is unconsciously plotting their downfall. However much his narrative seeks to temper their appalling conduct, it blackens them unwittingly in the very act of doing so. There are thus several possible versions of what Thady is up to. The reader is not allowed to decide among them.

A third-person, omniscient narration is a kind of meta-language, meaning that in realist fiction at least it cannot be an object of criticism or commentary within the narrative itself. Since this is the voice of the story itself, it seems impossible to call it into question. The only way this might happen is when a narrative pauses to reflect on itself. A renowned example of this occurs when George Eliot holds up the story of *Adam Bede* to insert a chapter in which she ponders certain questions of realism, the nature of character, the fictional presentation of low-life men and women and so on. This, so to speak, is the novel reflecting on the novel. There can be no such meta-language or authorial voice-over in so-called epistolary novels, which consist of letters written by the characters to each other. Neither can there be in most forms of drama, where what we hear is the speech of the characters rather than of the work itself. Ben Jonson cannot intervene to tell us what to make of Volpone, as Thackeray speaks up in *Vanity Fair* to point out that one of the book's most lovable characters is a halfwit.

This can make it hard to know what viewpoints a play itself endorses, and which it rejects. Take as an example Portia's celebrated speech about mercy in Shakespeare's *The Merchant of Venice*:

> *The quality of mercy is not strain'd;*
> *It droppeth as the gentle rain from heaven*
> *Upon the place beneath. It is twice blessed:*
> *It blesseth him that gives and him that takes.*
> *'Tis mightiest in the mightiest; it becomes*
> *The throned monarch better than his crown . . .*

It is hard not to be persuaded by such eloquence. Yet Portia's speech is considerably more self-interested than it may seem. She is intent on rescuing one of her own kind, the Venetian Christian Antonio, from the clutches of Shylock, an odious Jew. The Christians of the city have not been notable for showing mercy to this contemptible outsider, and will penalise him harshly when he loses his lawsuit against them. Now, however, they are begging Shylock through Portia, their self-appointed spokeswoman, to let the viscerally anti-Semitic Antonio off the hook. If they want Shylock to show mercy, it is because they are not prepared to grant him justice. Shylock has a legal document in his hand which states that he may carve a pound of flesh from Antonio's body; and though this may be a barbarous bargain, the pound of flesh is his due under law. Antonio, moreover, agreed to the deal. He even reckoned it a reasonable one in the circumstances.

If Shylock's stubborn clinging to the letter of the law seems legalistic, so is the ruse by which Portia triumphs over him, by pointing out that his bond permits him to take flesh but not blood. No actual court would allow such an outrageous quibble. The law must work according to common understandings, not duplicitous nitpicking. In any case, mercy may not be strained (constrained), but justice surely is. Punishments, for example, must be proportionate to crimes. To be merciful is indeed a virtue, but it must not be allowed to make a mockery of justice. There are several reasons for suspecting that there is more to this affair than Portia's setpiece speech would suggest. Yet because we have no voice-over to tell us what to think, we are left to draw our own conclusions.

There is a similar problem with Polonius' advice to his son Laertes in *Hamlet*, which ends with the much quoted lines 'This above all – to thine own self be true, / And it must follow, as the night the day, / Thou canst not then be false to any man.' Is this really sage counsel? What if you are a natural-born con man and decide to be true to your nature? There is no way of knowing what Shakespeare himself thought about this piece of paternal guidance. It has a sententious air about it that may strike some readers as authoritative. On the other hand, Polonius sometimes comes up with portentous statements which are of dubious value. Perhaps the play is simply poking fun at him, as it so often does. Or perhaps for a precious moment he swerves from his customary self-importance into a genuine moral insight. It is also possible that Shakespeare did not stop to ask himself whether he thought this advice was sound, or that he thought it was sound but was mistaken. Perhaps the case of the natural-born twister did not occur to him. We should not be afraid to impute failings to the Bard. His comedy, after all, hardly leaves us rolling in the aisles. We do not generally need to be carried out of *Twelfth Night* convulsed with hysterical laughter.

\* \* \*

Omniscient narrators need not go unchallenged. We may suspect that they have their own biases and blind spots. Take, for example, the relations between narratives and their characters. A novel might unduly idealise one of its characters, just as it might angle its storyline unduly in favour of a certain standpoint. Works of fiction can reveal attitudes to the characters and events they portray, either explicitly or implicitly, which a reader might want to question. An astute critic once commented that Scobie, the protagonist of Graham Greene's *The Heart of the Matter*, is both more and less admirable than the novel itself seems to think. We do not have to take a piece of fiction's own word as gospel, even though we have no words but its own. If a novel tells us that its heroine has green-flecked eyes, it is hard to quarrel with the claim. If it also suggests that she is the most black-hearted female since Lucretia Borgia, we might want to query this on the basis of what it shows of her, as opposed to what it says. A work of fiction may seem to believe that its characters are thick skulled, tender hearted or downright despicable, but it might always be mistaken. Unknown to itself, it might provide us with evidence against these judgements.

D.H. Lawrence's *Sons and Lovers* may serve as an example. The novel contains some tacit criticism of its protagonist Paul Morel, but nonetheless sees the world largely from his point of view. There is a secret complicity between the narrative and its central figure. In fact, there are times when the story seems to think more highly of its hero than we do. Since the world is seen largely in Paul's own terms, his lover, Miriam, is not handed enough of the script. We would be intrigued to learn more of her view of Paul, but are allowed no access to it. The narrative, so to speak, is stacked against her. It is prejudiced in its very structure, as the real-life Miriam was not slow to point out. The same might be said of Lawrence's *Lady Chatterley's Lover*, which refuses to hand the microphone to the cold-blooded Clifford Chatterley. Instead, he is presented almost entirely from the outside. We might contrast this with Tolstoy's sensitive treatment of the unappetising figure of Karenin in *Anna Karenina*. It also differs sharply from Lawrence's treatment of Gerald Crich in *Women in Love*. Gerald represents much that his author finds abhorrent, but he is superbly well realised all the same. He is shown from the inside, in so far as he has any spiritual inside to be shown. Clifford Chatterley, by contrast, is reduced to a stereotype so that the novel may write him off with a minimum of effort. He is also disabled, and Lawrence is not at his most admirable when dealing with people in wheelchairs.

George Eliot's *Adam Bede* allows the reader some access to the inner life of Hetty Sorrel, a young working woman who is seduced by the lascivious local squire, has an illegitimate child as a result, kills the baby and ends up having to be rescued from the gallows. A good deal of this high drama is presented from the outside, as though Hetty lacks the kind of inner depths that might prove worth plumbing. She is more an object of pity than a full-blooded tragic figure. Her surname 'Sorrel' suggests sorrow, but it also means a kind of horse, which is not quite as respectful. The narrative finally packs Hetty off into exile, thus clearing the way for Adam, the hero of the piece, to choose a rather more high-minded wife than this empty-headed milkmaid. There is no such one-sidedness in Eliot's finest novel, *Middlemarch*, in which the narrator behaves like a judicious chairperson in a public debate, ensuring that all the characters have their say. Even the bloodless Casaubon must be shown as a feeling, suffering creature. There is no hogging the microphone here.

There is a parallel to Eliot's treatment of Casaubon in *Jude the Obscure*. The novel encourages us to feel a degree of distaste for the staid, conventionally minded Phillotson, to whom, as we have seen, the free-thinking Sue Bridehead is miserably married. Sue begs her husband for her freedom, yet just as we are expecting this eminently respectable citizen to refuse her, he surprises us by conceding that she is free to go. He does this despite his regard for public opinion, and despite his deep personal dismay at the loss of the woman he loves. The result of his selfless action is that he also loses his job as a schoolmaster. It is part of the novel's own rebuff to convention that it refuses to make a bogeyman out of this unprepossessing figure. Instead, it allows him a dignified, generous response to his wife's unhappiness. Lawrence would probably have granted him no such magnanimity. He might scarcely have allowed him an inner life at all.

In this sense, Hardy's characters can surprise us, in a way that Austen's or Dickens's rarely do. They can leap suddenly out of windows, marry a man they physically detest, sit motionless for long periods up a tree, unravel their underwear to rescue someone trapped on a cliff, sell their wife at a fair on a sudden whim, or engage in a virtuoso exhibition of sword fighting for no very obvious reason. Jude drunkenly recites the Nicene creed in an Oxford pub, hardly a regular occurrence in one's local cocktail bar. Hardy's novels do not seem particularly embarrassed by the lack of realism of such events, or even particularly to notice it. They are content to allow different kinds of fiction, realist and non-realist, to sit cheek by jowl within their covers, without trying to force them into a single mode.

Hardy's treatment of Tess Durbeyfield in *Tess of the D'Urbervilles* makes a telling contrast with George Eliot's handling of Hetty Sorrel. Hardy is clearly in love with his heroine, rather in the way that Samuel Richardson is in love with Clarissa, and aims to do justice to this much abused young woman. In this sense, the narrative can be seen as making loving amends to Tess for the way some of its own characters shamefully exploit her. It tries to present her as a whole woman, rather than idealise her like Angel Clare or sensualise her like Alec D'Urberville.

It is a generous-spirited effort, though not without its problems. If the book tries to depict Tess from the inside, it also makes her the object of its own amorous gaze, exhibiting her for the reader's similar inspection. As critics have pointed out, the story finds it hard to bring its heroine into focus. It tries to make her transparent, but finds itself shifting from one voice or viewpoint to another in its effort to see her clearly. There is something about her sexuality which defeats representation. At critical points in the narrative, such as the moment of her seduction, Tess's consciousness is inaccessible to the reader. She resists the way the (implicitly male) narrator tries to appropriate her. Conflicting, even contradictory views of her overlap, without being resolved into a coherent whole. In trying to display her character, the novel succeeds only in destabilising our sense of her. The book is full of images of pricking, piercing and penetrating, as though the narrator has erotic fantasies of possessing his protagonist to the full. In the end, however, she is not to be pinned down.

Entire novels can treat their subject-matter with notable bias. Charles Dickens's *Hard Times*, for example, paints a partisan view of Coketown, the north-of-England industrial town in which the novel's action is set. The place itself is viewed impressionistically, as though by a south-of-England observer glimpsing it from a train. The novel's hero is Stephen Blackpool, a deferential, morally conscientious working man. We are invited to admire the way he refuses to cave in to trade union pressure during a strike, but the truth is that Stephen has very little political consciousness at all. He is remote from his fellow workers for personal reasons, not political ones. He dies in solitude, and the general impression is that he ends his life as a martyr to the bigotry of organised labour. Yet his death actually has no political significance whatsoever.

The novel portrays the labour movement as loud mouthed, sectarian and potentially violent. In doing so, it writes off one of the few forces in Victorian Britain which challenged the very social injustices it is so indignant about. The strike in the novel is based on a real-life one, and Dickens paints a far more sympathetic portrait of the event in his journalism than he does in his novel. In fact, he commends what he sees as the self-restraint of the striking workers. *Hard Times* also delivers a savage caricature of Utilitarianism, a creed which was actually responsible for some vital social reforms in Dickens's England. The founder of the movement, Jeremy Bentham, was opposed to the criminalisation of homosexuality, an astonishingly enlightened position for someone of his time. Utilitarianism involved a lot more than making a fetish out of facts, which is the way the book crassly presents it. Since some of Dickens's best friends were Utilitarians, it is hard to believe that he could not have been aware of this distortion.

A story may take up no attitude to its subject-matter even when we might expect it to. This is true of Evelyn Waugh's satirical novel *Decline and Fall*, which uses its hero, Paul Pennyfeather, as a focus for the antics of English high society. Because he is simply a point of entry into this world, Pennyfeather is not meant to be a well-rounded character. He is just a kind of blank at the novel's centre, as lightweight as the name Pennyfeather would suggest. He does not seem able to evaluate his own experience at all. In a superb piece of black comedy, he is sentenced to seven years' penal servitude as a scapegoat for someone else's crimes of prostitution and white slave traffic. Yet he fails to voice anything remotely approaching a protest against this grotesque piece of injustice.

Paul's blankness is one way in which he belongs to the shallow high society world around him. It thus reflects on that world rather badly. But it also serves to stop Paul from criticising it. The fact that its hero is little more than a cipher is part of the rich comedy of the book, but it also prevents him from questioning the behaviour of his upper-class cronies. The novel's attitude to these characters is scrupulously neutral, and this deadpan treatment adds to its funniness. It is a kind of literary equivalent of the stiff upper lip, as the most shocking, surreal occurrences are reported with off-hand indifference. Yet this neutrality of tone is also highly convenient for a writer like Waugh, a man with strong upper-class sympathies.

Waugh's comedy works partly by emptying people of their inner lives. Yet it may be his characters do not have much inner life to be emptied of in the first place. This serves to show up their moral flimsiness, and thus counts against them. If they are really as vacuous as they appear, however, it is hard to see how they can be held responsible for their scandalous behaviour, which counts in their favour. Paradoxically, what is most to be criticised about these drones and loungers – that they are mere paper-thin personalities – is also what makes them most immune to criticism.

There are various ways in which narratives can load the dice in their own favour. George Orwell's *Animal Farm* is about a group of animals who take over their farm and try to run it themselves, with disastrous results. As such, the novel is meant to be an allegory of the collapse of socialist democracy in the early Soviet Union. Yet the fact is that animals are incapable of running farms. It is hard to sign cheques or ring up your suppliers when you have hoofs rather than hands. It is true that this is not why the animals' experiment fails, but it has an unconscious influence on the reader's response to it. So the story is slanted from the outset. The way it sets up its terms helps to prove its point. The allegory might also imply, no doubt against its leftist author's intentions, that working people are too stupid to manage their own affairs. The title of the book, incidentally, can be read as ironic. 'Animal' and 'Farm' go naturally together. But they do not go together here.

The cards are similarly stacked in William Golding's *Lord of the Flies*, which shows a bunch of schoolboys on a desert island gradually reverting to barbarism. Among other things, this is supposed to illustrate the case that civilisation is only skin-deep. As in Joseph Conrad's *Heart of Darkness*, we are all barbarians under the skin, a view which effectively puts paid to any hope of social progress. Scratch a schoolboy and you find a savage. Yet choosing children for your characters helps to make the point rather too conveniently. Children are only semi-socialised in any case. They are not yet capable of such complex operations as running their own communities. In fact, some of them are not much more advanced in this respect than Orwell's pigs. It is not surprising that the social order they try to build on the island rapidly breaks down. *Lord of the Flies* thus makes things rather too easy for itself. The way it sets up its case makes it more plausible than it might otherwise appear. It may be that men and women are fallen, corrupted creatures, as Golding himself believed; but you cannot prove the point by showing a group of frightened schoolchildren failing to evolve the equivalent of the United Nations.

There may be discrepancies between what a narrative shows and what it says. A particularly blatant example of this can be found in John Milton's *Paradise Lost*, when Adam decides to share Eve's fate by sharing the death-dealing apple. From the way the poem presents the event, there is no doubt that he makes his decision out of love for his partner:

> *no. no! I feel*
> *The link of nature draw me: flesh of flesh,*
> *Bone of my bone thou art, and from thy state*
> *Mine never shall be parted, bliss or woe.*

Adam is ready to risk his own life out of loyalty to Eve. Yet when he himself comes to eat the apple, the tone of the verse changes sharply:

> *he scrupled not to eat,*
> *Against his better knowledge, not deceived,*
> *But fondly overcome with female charm.*

'Fondly overcome with female charm' is a flagrant distortion of Adam's state of mind, as the poem itself has just portrayed it. ('Fondly' here means 'foolishly'.) It reduces his courageous self-sacrifice to the lure of a pretty face. As Adam takes the apple, ready to lay down his life alongside his lover, the poem abruptly abandons all sympathy for him. Instead, it adopts a severely juridical tone. It insists that he is performing this action freely, without self-deception, in full knowledge of its catastrophic consequences.

Milton the theologian takes over from Milton the humanist, as doctrine gets the better of drama.

There are similar conflicts between what we see and what we are told in the fiction of Daniel Defoe. Defoe's novels are fascinated by the workaday material world. What we find in his writing is a kind of pure narrativity, in which the overriding question is always 'What comes next?' Events are important in so far as they lead to other events. These restless narratives plunge forward without much sense of overall design. There is no logical conclusion or natural closure to Defoe's tales. They accumulate narrative for its own sake, as a capitalist accumulates profit for its own sake. It is as though the desire to narrate is insatiable. In a world where to stop is to stagnate, you settle down only to take off again, and with Defoe this is true both of the narrative and of the characters themselves. Robinson Crusoe is no sooner home from his island than he is off on his travels once more, stockpiling further adventures which he promises to share with us in the future. Characters like Moll Flanders move so fast, swapping one husband for another and hopping from one form of petty crime to the next, that they seem to have no continuous identity. Instead, they live off the top of their heads, by the skin of their teeth and (literally in Moll's case) by the seat of their pants.

Defoe clearly relishes realism for its own sake. As James Joyce once said of himself, he has the mind of a grocer. In fact, the English novel takes off at the point where everyday existence begins to seem endlessly enthralling. This was hardly true of the literary forms which preceded it: tragedy, epic, elegy, pastoral, romance and the like. Genres like this deal in deities, high-born characters and extraordinary events. They are not much interested in prostitutes and pickpockets. The idea of allowing a whore like

Moll Flanders to tell the story would be as unthinkable as allowing a giraffe to narrate it. For a Christian Dissenter like Defoe, however, savouring everyday life for its own sake is not morally acceptable, even though his fiction does just that. The material world is supposed to point to the spiritual one. It is not to be treated as an end in itself. Real events must be scanned for a moral or religious meaning. So Defoe assures us in the style of a tabloid journalist that he is reporting these sensational happenings (theft, bigamy, fraud, fornication and so on) only so that we can learn a moral lesson from them. Yet this is conspicuously not the case. The story and the moral are absurdly at odds with each other. We are invited to believe that human history is guided by divine Providence, but nothing could be more implausible. History is just a chapter of accidents. It is driven by voracious self-interest, not shaped by some moral design. Virtue is for those who can afford it. What the novels say does not fit with what they show.

D.H. Lawrence objected to writers who, as he comments in his *Study of Thomas Hardy*, 'put their thumb in the pan'. He meant by this that a work of fiction is a balance of forces with a mysteriously autonomous life of its own, and an author should not disturb this delicate equilibrium by forcing his own purposes upon it. Tolstoy, he thought, had done just this, unforgivably, in killing off his own great creation Anna Karenina. This 'Judas' of an author, as Lawrence calls him, had taken fright at the magnificent flourish of life that was his heroine, and had cravenly disposed of her by pushing her under a train. Writers who allowed their protagonists to go under were in Lawrence's eyes simply 'doing dirt on life'. It followed for him that tragedy was something of a cop-out. In fact, he stands out among the major modernist authors in his aversion to it. Characters in Lawrence who cannot attain fulfilment are not generally to be seen as tragic. They are to be swept out of the way so that others may find their own fulfilment unimpeded.

Lawrence may be wrong about Tolstoy and tragedy, but he is right to see that authors quite often rig their narratives to suit their fictional purposes. Just when Dorothea Brooke, the heroine of George Eliot's *Middlemarch*, seems trapped in a loveless marriage with a withered old pedant, the novel itself steps in and polishes him off with a fatal heart attack. The modern form of Providence, in other words, is known as fiction. *Jane Eyre* is anxious to marry its heroine off to Rochester, who is already married; so it topples his mad wife off a blazing rooftop to her death. If characters themselves are reluctant to commit murder, the narrative itself may always step in and oblige. Narratives are like hired assassins, ready to do the dirty work that their characters may flinch from. David Copperfield's childish, rather vacant-headed wife Dora is clearly an unsuitable partner for him, and so is obviously not going to make it to the end of the novel. She is as doomed as the domineering businessman who rides roughshod over his fellow characters at the start of a detective story, and who is clearly going to end up with a knife in his guts.

A story may step in to save the day with a timely legacy, the arrival of an eligible bachelor in the district, or the discovery of a long-lost, seriously rich relative. It is the task of realist narratives of this kind to grant the virtuous their reward and the villains their comeuppance. They must rectify the blunders of reality. Sometimes, as in the work of Henry Fielding, this is done with an ironic sense of its artifice. In real life, a novel may slyly intimate, the hero would probably have been hanged; but since this is fiction it is obligatory to hand him an adoring wife and a sizeable landed estate. If he himself is shown actively working for such things, this will diminish our sense of his virtue. Virtue is not supposed to be self-regarding. So the plot has to go to work on his behalf. Fielding allows Tom Jones to achieve happiness, while warning us that such felicitous outcomes are untypical of real life. There is, he remarks in the course of the novel, a worthy moral doctrine that the good will receive their reward in this world – a doctrine, he adds, which has only one defect, namely that it is not true.

In a similar way, the depraved and black-hearted are usually worsted by the end of the story. Their schemes are foiled, their fortunes are snatched from their hairy paws, and they are packed off to prison or married off to monsters. The poor are filled with good things, while the rich are sent empty away. Yet in real life, so it is discreetly hinted, the villains would probably have ended up as judges and cabinet ministers. There is a similar sense of irony at the end of some of Shakespeare's comedies, which make us wryly aware that this is probably not how things would have panned out in reality. *A Midsummer Night's Dream* concludes with the 'right' couples being married off to each other, but not before the play has called into question the whole idea of rightness when it comes to sexual attraction. Instead, it demonstrates how anyone can desire anyone else – how there is an anarchic quality about desire which is a threat to an orderly plot. The queen of the fairies even falls in love with a donkey, which is not the only time that a royal personage has done so. In *The Tempest*, Prospero can be reconciled with his enemies only by deploying magical devices. Charlotte Brontë's novel *Villette* supplies us with alternative endings, one comic and one tragic. 'Here's your happy ending if you insist on one,' it seems to murmur to the reader, 'but don't imagine that it's necessarily the truth of the matter.'

Henry James, who was unafraid of tragic outcomes, writes sardonically in his essay 'The Art of Fiction' of the 'distribution at the last of prizes, pensions, husbands, wives, babies, millions, appended paragraphs, and cheerful remarks' which we find in the final pages of so many realist novels. The point of such conclusions is to console, whereas the effect of many a modernist ending is to unsettle. The Victorians believed that one of the functions of art was to raise the reader's spirits. Gloom was regarded as morally debilitating. It could even be seen as politically dangerous. A dispirited people was a disaffected one. This is one reason why almost all Victorian novels end on an affirmative note. Even the work that sails nearest to outright tragedy, *Wuthering Heights*, manages to pull off a tentatively positive conclusion. These happy endings are really fantasies, and fantasy, as Freud remarked, is 'a correction of an unsatisfying reality'. We know that in the real world the distribution of benefits leaves something to be desired. Admirable women get loutish husbands, crooked bankers stay out of prison and cute little babies are born to white supremacists. So a spot of poetic justice does not come amiss. Perhaps the novel is one of the few remaining places where such justice is possible. It is not a particularly consoling thought.

In an essay on Henry James in his *Notes on Life and Letters*, Joseph Conrad speaks of conventional fictional endings in terms of 'solution by rewards and punishments, by crowned love, by fortune, by a broken leg or a sudden death'. 'These solutions,' he continues, 'are legitimate inasmuch as they satisfy the desire for finality, for which our hearts yearn, with a longing greater than a longing for the loaves and fishes of this earth. Perhaps the only true desire of mankind, coming thus to light in its hours of leisure, is to be set at rest.' This hunger for closure, this constant cry of 'What happens in the end?', keeps us eagerly reading. It is one reason we are so entranced by thrillers, mysteries, cliff-hangers and Gothic horror stories. Not long after Conrad wrote these words, Sigmund Freud would call our craving for finality the death drive.

Yet if we want our curiosity to be satisfied, we are also wary of such fulfilment. If the pleasures of closure come too soon, they ruin the delights of suspense. We long for assurance, but we also desire to defer it. We need to be gratified, but we also revel in the anxiety of not knowing. Unless a solution is temporarily withdrawn, there can be no story. It is its absence which keeps the narrative going. Yet we hanker for it to be restored, like a lost puppy or the Garden of Eden. When the narrator of Conrad's *Heart of Darkness* meets Kurtz's bereaved mistress at the end of the tale, he tells her a consoling untruth. It is as though she is treated by the story as a traditional audience in search of a happy ending. Conrad himself, however, suspects not only that endings are rarely happy, but that there are no definitive endings in any case.

\* \* \*

We have seen already that stories are possible because some initial order is disrupted. A snake sidles into the happy garden, a stranger arrives in town, Don Quixote sallies forth on the open road, Lovelace takes a fancy to Clarissa, Tom Jones is pitched out of his patron's country mansion, Lord Jim makes a fatal jump and Josef K is arrested for a nameless crime. In a good many realist novels, the point of the ending is to restore this order, perhaps in an enriched form. The original sin results in a state of conflict and chaos, but this will finally be redeemed. Like the Fall from Eden, it is a *felix culpa* or fortunate fault, since without it there would be no story. The reader is accordingly consoled and uplifted. He is assured that there is a logic implicit in reality, and that the task of the novel is to bring it patiently to light. We are all part of a stupendous plot, and the good news is that this plot has a comic outcome.

It may be helpful in this respect to think of narrative as a kind of strategy. Like any strategy, it mobilises certain resources and deploys certain techniques to achieve specific goals. A good many realist novels can be seen as problem-solving devices. They create problems for themselves which they then seek to resolve. Human beings who do this may find themselves being referred to psychiatrists, but it is the kind of thing we expect of realist fiction. If there is to be narrative suspense, however, difficulties must not be cleared up too quickly. Emma Woodhouse must end up in Mr Knightley's arms, but not in the second paragraph. In resolving one kind of problem, however, literary works may simply succeed in throwing up another, which needs to be tackled in its turn. Modernist and postmodernist literary works are generally less interested in solutions. Their aim is rather to lay bare certain problems. They do not typically end with fast-living fraudsters being hung upside down from lamp posts, or a set of blissful marriages. And in this, one might suggest, they are more realistic than most realism.

For classical realism, the world itself is story-shaped. In a lot of modernist fiction, by contrast, there is no order apart from what we ourselves construct. And since any such order is arbitrary, so are fictional openings and endings. There are no divinely ordained origins or natural closures. Which is to say that there are no logical middles either. What may count as an end for you may serve as an origin for me. You can make a start or call a halt wherever you want. Ends and origins are not inherent in the world. It is you, not the world, who calls the shots in this respect. Wherever you make a start, however, you may be sure that an enormous amount will have happened already. And wherever you call a halt, a great deal will carry on regardless.

Some modernist works are thus sceptical of the whole notion of narrative. Narrative suggests that there is a shapeliness to the world, an orderly procession of causes and effects. It is sometimes (though by no means always) bound up with a faith in progress, the power of reason and the forward march of humanity. It would not be too fanciful to claim that narrative of this classical kind fell to pieces on the battlefields of the First World War, an event which scarcely fostered a faith in human reason. It was around these years that the great modernist works were produced, from *Ulysses* and *The Waste Land* to Yeats's *The Wild Swans at Coole* and Lawrence's *Women in Love*. For the modernist mind, reality does not evolve in a tidy fashion. Event A may lead to event B, but it also leads to events C, D, E and countless others. It is the product of countless factors as well. Who is to decide which of these storylines should take priority? Whereas realism views the world as an unfolding, modernism tends to see it as a text. The word 'text' here is akin to 'textile', meaning something spun of many interwoven threads. On this view, reality is less a logical development than a tangled web, in which every component is intricately caught up with every other. There is no centre to such a web, and no foundation on which it rests. You cannot pinpoint where it begins or ends. There is no event A or Z. The process can be unravelled back endlessly and unfolds infinitely. In the beginning was the word, as St John's Gospel declares; but a word is only a word because of its relations to other words. So for the first word to be a word, there must have been at least one other word already. Which is to say that there was no first word. If it makes sense to speak of language being born, then, as the anthropologist Claude Lévi-Strauss has put it, it must have been born 'at a stroke'.

So the idea of narrative is thrown into crisis. For modernism, knowing where something began, even if this were possible, will not necessarily yield you the truth about it. To assume so is to be guilty of what has been called the genetic fallacy. There is no one grand narrative, simply a host of mini-narratives, each of which may have its partial truth. One can give any number of accounts of even the most humble aspect of reality, not all of which will be mutually compatible. It is impossible to know what trifling incident in a story might prove momentous in the end, rather as for the biologists it is hard to know which lowly form of life might evolve in the fullness of time into something exceptional. Who, contemplating a slimy, self-involved little mollusc billions of years ago, would have imagined the emergence of Tom Cruise? Stories try to foist some design on this weblike world, but in doing so they succeed only in simplifying and impoverishing it. To narrate is to falsify. In fact, one might even claim that to write is to falsify. Writing, after all, is a process which unfolds in time, and in this respect resembles narrative. The only authentic literary work, then, would be one which is conscious of this falsification, and which tries to tell its tale in a way that takes it into account.

This is to say that all narratives must be ironic. They must deliver their accounts while keeping their own limitations constantly in mind. They must somehow incorporate what they do not know into what they know. The limits of the story must become part of the story. This is one reason why some of Conrad's narrators, or the storyteller of Ford Madox Ford's *The Good Soldier*, are at pains to acknowledge their own blind spots. It is as though the nearest one can come to the truth is a confession of one's inevitable ignorance. Narratives must find a way of suggesting that there could be many versions of their subject-matter beside their own. If they are not to appear deceptively absolute, they must point to their own arbitrariness. Samuel Beckett sometimes sets out on one tall tale, aborts it almost as soon as it is off the ground, then launches an equally pointless one in its place.

Modern storytelling, in other words, has lost the kind of necessity it had in the days when poets would recount the mythical origins of the tribe or sing its military victories. Now, telling a tale has become gratuitous. It has no foundation in reality, as the origins of the tribe or the history of the nation are supposed to have. So stories have to be self-sustaining. They can appeal to no authority but their own, unlike the author of Genesis or Dante's *Divine Comedy*. This gives the storyteller a lot more room to manoeuvre. But it is a negative kind of freedom. We live in a world in which there is nothing that cannot be narrated, but nothing that needs to be either.

There are narratives which have stringent limits but which do not seem aware of the fact. Elizabeth Gaskell's novel *Mary Barton* is a case in point. Its male protagonist, John Barton, is a down-at-heel industrial worker in Victorian Manchester who becomes a political militant. When he does so, however, he seems to disappear beyond the horizon of the story, or at least beyond its comprehension. He can be felt lurking on its margins, but is no longer seen head-on. The novel even seems uncertain as to what kind of activist he is, whether a Chartist, a communist or otherwise. And if the book itself does not know, then nobody does. Barton has entered a shadowy world into which the story he appears in, with its own more conventional political views, simply cannot follow him. It is significant in this respect that Gaskell originally intended to call the novel after its protagonist, but changed her mind and called it after his less disreputable daughter Mary instead.

With the advent of modernism, then, it is becoming increasingly difficult to tell even the simplest of tales straight. Take the case of Joseph Conrad, who as a former seaman is renowned for his ability to spin a rattling good yarn. *Heart of Darkness* is among other things a gripping detective story. Yet as the fable unfolds, it begins to blur, dissolve and crumble at the edges. The story is told in a vividly concretising style, but there is an aura of mistiness about it which no degree of meticulous detail can dispel. Marlow, the protagonist, does not seem to be getting anywhere. As he moves upriver into the centre of Africa he is also journeying deeper inside himself, into some timeless realm of myth and the unconscious. So his journey is more inward than forward. At the same time, as he sails away from civilisation towards so-called savagery, he is travelling into the primeval past. To push forward into the heart of Africa is to revert to the 'primitive' origins of humanity. So the narrative moves forward and backward at the same time. Progress is purely illusory. There is no hope in history. History, to adapt the words of Joyce's Stephen Dedalus, is a nightmare from which modernism is trying to awaken. If Conrad's narrative is in trouble, it is partly because the nineteenth-century belief in progress – of a continuous upward trek from barbarism to civilisation – has taken an almighty battering.

It therefore comes as no surprise that Kurtz, the monstrously depraved figure whom Marlow is in search of, first came to Africa as 'an emissary of pity, and science, and progress, and devil knows what else'. (One might expect that last phrase to read 'and *the* devil knows what else', but English was not Conrad's native language, and his prose sometimes reminds us of the fact.) Kurtz, a colonial

official, arrived in Africa as a champion of progress and enlighten-
ment, and has now degenerated into a man who performs certain
'unspeakable rites' and secret abominations. Having come to
enlighten the inhabitants of the Belgian Congo, he now wants to
exterminate them. So the progressive reverts to the primitive in the
content of the story, as well as in its form.

Neither history nor narrative seems to get you anywhere any
more. Joyce's Leopold Bloom gets up, potters rather pointlessly
around Dublin and returns home. Linear notions of history give
way to cyclical ones. Stories are forever trying to net down truths
that prove elusive. To tell a tale is to try to shape the void. It is as
futile as ploughing the ocean. Marlow in *Heart of Darkness* is literally telling his story in the dark, unsure whether he has an audience
as he squats on the ship's deck at night. As we have seen already, his
final spoken words are a lie. George Eliot and Thomas Hardy are
convinced that the truth is essentially narratable, whereas Conrad
and Woolf have no such faith. For them, truth lies beyond representation. It can be shown but not stated. Perhaps Kurtz has had
a terrifying glimpse of it, but it cannot be crammed into the
straitjacket of a story. There is a heart of darkness at the centre of
every yarn.

It may be that Marlow can recite his tale only because he has
failed to arrive at the truth, and never will. A piece of fiction that
managed to pronounce the final word about the human condition
would have nothing left to say. It would simply trail off into silence.
It would perish of the truth it presented. 'Are not our lives too
short,' Marlow asks, 'for that full utterance which through all our
stammering is of course our only and abiding intention?' What
keeps narrative on the move is its sheer impossibility. The truth
that (modernist) stories pursue lies beyond the limits of language;

yet they refuse to give up on it all the same, and it is this refusal that keeps storytelling in business. One is always nearer by not standing still. Marlow speaks in *Heart of Darkness* of travelling to 'the farthest point of navigation and the culminating point of my experience'. The only question is whether, having arrived at this stark extremity, one has the courage like Kurtz to peer over the edge into the abyss. Kurtz has journeyed beyond language and narrative into an obscene reality far beyond their frontiers; and this is presented by the story as a kind of horrific triumph. He has stared the Medusa's head in the face without flinching, and this, perhaps, is a more admirable achievement than suburban middle-class virtue. It is a familiar modernist case, as audacious as it is dangerous.

This, at least, is what Marlow himself believes about Kurtz, a man who hardly makes an appearance in the book. But he might always be falsely idealising him. Conrad himself may have other opinions. Some of his other works, like *Lord Jim* and *Nostromo*, are equally shy of telling a story straight. Instead, their accounts loop back on themselves, start off halfway through, run several storylines at the same time, exchange one narrator for another or recount the same events from different standpoints. The reader is forced to slice into the story at one angle and then another, skating backward and forward in time and relying on someone's record of someone's account of someone else's report.

Some of this is reminiscent of one of the greatest of English comic masterpieces, the eighteenth-century author Laurence Sterne's *Tristram Shandy*. Garbling one's storytelling is not confined to modernism. Sterne's novel is really a narrative about the impossibility of narrative, at least of a realist kind. What it has seen is that realism, strictly speaking, is beyond our power. No piece of writing can simply tell it as it is. All so-called realism is an angled, edited version of reality. There is no 'complete' account possible of a tiny stain on one's fingernail, let alone of a human life. The realist novel is meant to reflect existence as it is, in all its unruly detail; but it is also supposed to mould this formless stuff into a shapely narrative. And these two aims are really incompatible. Any story is bound to select, revise and exclude, and so fail to give us the unvarnished truth. If it tried to do that, it would have to go on for ever. One thing would lead to another and that to another, in a series of digressions upon digressions. Which is exactly what happens in *Tristram Shandy*.

For Sterne (or so at least he pretends), selecting and excluding is a way of cheating the reader. Design is really deceit. So Tristram, the book's narrator, sets out to tell us everything he possibly can about his birth and upbringing. The result of this apparently reader-friendly gesture is that the narrative rapidly stalls and the reader is utterly bamboozled. We suspect that what may look reader-friendly may be secretly mischief-making. By trying to tell us everything about himself, all the way back to the moment of his conception, Tristram ends up spinning such an unwieldy mass of text that we risk being completely flummoxed. The whole enterprise is hilariously self-undoing. It is not long before we begin to suspect that the hero is out of his mind, and feel ourselves being dragged in much the same direction.

Realism appears to give us the world in all its delightful or alarming dishevelledness, but it actually does no such thing. If a telephone rings in a realist novel or a naturalistic drama, it is almost certain to be a move in the plot rather than a wrong number. Realist works choose the kind of characters, events and situations which will help to build up their moral vision. In order to conceal this selectivity, however, and thus to preserve their air of reality, they usually supply us with a lot of detail that really is pretty random. They might tell us that a brain surgeon who puts in a brief appearance has huge, hairy hands, whereas she might easily have been equipped with smooth, dainty ones with no loss to the storyline. The detail is entirely arbitrary. It is there simply to fabricate a sense of the real. A realist novel may have its heroine hail a maroon-coloured taxi, whereas an experimental novel might make the taxi maroon on one page, no colour at all on another, and with a driver made entirely out of marzipan on a third. In doing so, it would deliberately let the realist cat out of the bag. It would expose to view what the realist novel gets up to behind our backs. This, in effect, is the aim of *Tristram Shandy*. No sooner had the novel form emerged in Britain than it was deviously deconstructed.

Tristram's purpose is to write his autobiography. Yet if he is not to deceive the reader he must leave nothing out, with the result that he never gets his story beyond childhood. After completing two sizeable volumes of the work, he has still not got himself born. After nine volumes, we do not even know what he looks like. To recount his life-history, he is forever having to nip from one time-stream to another, double back to clarify a point, or hold up one part of narrative while he gets on with another bit. His history, he remarks, 'is digressive, and it is progressive too – and at the very same time'. He must also keep a vigilant eye on what one might call the reader's time-stream, urging us to slow down or speed up as the case may be. Strictly speaking, the hero would need to stop living while he was writing, otherwise he would never be able to catch up with himself. The more he writes, the more he will have to write, since the more living he will have done in the meanwhile. For the sake of completeness, he would also have to include the act of writing his life-history in his life-history.

As Tristram scribbles busily away, the whole novel gradually comes apart in his hands. The narrative logjams, bits fall off, characters are left standing at doors for the duration of several chapters, details begin to spawn uncontrollably, a Preface and a Dedication get displaced, and the author himself threatens to sink without trace under his potentially infinite pile of text. Storytelling is an absurd enterprise. It is an attempt to put in sequential form a reality which is not sequential at all. So is language itself. To say one thing necessarily means excluding another, even for *Finnegans Wake*. The very medium in which Tristram tries to grasp the truth of his identity – words – succeeds only in obscuring it.

Exorbitant claims are sometimes made for narrative. Historically speaking, it goes a long way back. Storytelling would seem as ancient as humanity itself. It is sometimes said that we speak, think, love, dream and act in narrative. This is true in one sense, since we are all creatures of time. Yet not all men and women experience their existence in this way. Some see their lives as a coherent story, while others do not. The same applies to different cultures. One thinks of the old joke 'My life contains some wonderful characters, but I can't work out the plot.' The hackneyed metaphor of life as a journey implies a sense of purpose and continuity which not everyone finds illuminating. Where exactly do people think they are going? A life can be significant without having a goal, just as a work of art can be. What is the purpose of having children or wearing shocking pink tights? Works of fiction like *Tristram Shandy*, *Heart of Darkness*, *Ulysses* and *Mrs Dalloway* can serve to free us from seeing human life as goal-driven, logically unfolding and rigorously coherent. As such, they can help us to enjoy it more.

\* \* \*

What, finally, of the difference between narrative and plot? One way to distinguish between the two is to think of the novels of Agatha Christie. Christie's crime thrillers are almost all plot. Other features of narrative – scene-setting, dialogue, atmosphere, symbolism, description, reflection, in-depth characteristion and so on – are ruthlessly stripped away to leave little but the bare bones of the action. The books differ in this respect from the detective fiction of Dorothy L. Sayers, P.D. James, Ruth Rendell and Ian Rankin, authors who have embed their plots in a much richer narrative context.

Plot, then, is part of narrative, but it does not exhaust it. We generally mean by it the significant action of a story. It signifies the way in which characters, events and situations are interconnected. Plot is the logic or inner dynamic of the narrative. For Aristotle's *Poetics*, it represents 'the combination of the incidents, or things done in the story'. A summary of it is what we tend to come up with when someone asks us what a story is about. The plot of *The Sound of Music* includes the Von Trapp family's flight from the Nazis, but not Julie Andrews warbling away on a mountain top or the fact that she has slightly prominent front teeth. The murder of Banquo is part of the plot of *Macbeth*, but not the speech 'Tomorrow and tomorrow and tomorrow . . .'.

There are plenty of plotless narratives, such as *Waiting for Godot*, 'Thirty Days Hath September' or Joyce's *A Portrait of the Artist as a Young Man*. There are also narratives which may or may not have plots, in the sense that we cannot be sure whether some significant action is afoot or not. This is sometimes the case in the fiction of Franz Kafka. It is also occasionally true of Henry James. Paranoiacs and conspiracy theorists are inclined to detect plots where there are none. They 'overread' stray details and random events, finding in them the signs of some sinisterly concealed narrative. Othello does this with Desdemona's handkerchief, which he misreads as a token of her sexual infidelity. It also happens in *The Book of Laughter and Forgetting* by Milan Kundera, who lived for some years under a Communist regime in Eastern Europe. Since such regimes are constantly spying on their citizens, perpetually on the look-out for the slightest flicker of dissidence, they qualify as paranoid. As with paranoia, nothing that happens can happen by accident. Everything must have some portentous significance. In Kundera's story, a character is being sick in the centre of communist Prague, and another character strolls up and gazes down at him. 'I know exactly what you mean,' he murmurs sympathetically.

# CHAPTER 4

# Interpretation

One of the things we mean by calling a piece of writing 'literary' is that it is not tied to a specific context. It is true that all literary works arise from particular conditions. Jane Austen's novels spring from the world of the English landed gentry of the eighteenth and early nineteenth century, while *Paradise Lost* has as its backdrop the English Civil War and its aftermath. Yet though these works emerge from such contexts, their meaning is not confined to them. Consider the difference between a poem and a manual for assembling a table lamp. The manual makes sense only in a specific, practical situation. Unless we are really starved for inspiration, we do not generally turn to it in order to reflect on the mystery of birth or the frailty of humankind. A poem, by contrast, can still be meaningful outside its original context, and may alter its meaning as it moves from one place or time to another. Like a baby, it is detached from its author as soon as it enters the world. All literary works are orphaned at birth. Rather as our parents do not continue to govern our lives as we grow up, so the poet cannot determine the situations in which his or her work will be read, or what sense we are likely to make of it.

What we call works of literature differ in this way from roadsigns and bus tickets. They are peculiarly 'portable', able to be carried from one location to another, which is true of bus tickets only for those intent on defrauding the bus company. They are less dependent for their meaning on the circumstances from which they arose. Rather, they are inherently open ended, which is one reason why they can be subject to a whole range of interpretations. It is also one reason why we tend to pay closer attention to their language than we do with bus tickets. We do not take their language primarily as practical. Instead, we assume that it is intended to have some value in itself.

This is not so true of everyday language. A panic-stricken shout of 'Man overboard!' is rarely ambiguous. We do not normally treat it as a delectable piece of wordplay. If we hear this cry while on board ship, we are unlikely to linger over the way the vowel-sound of 'board' rings a subtle change on the vowel-sound of 'Over', or note the fact that the stresses of the shout fall on the first and last syllables. Nor would we pause to read some symbolic meaning into it. We do not take the word 'Man' to signify humanity as such, or the whole phrase as suggestive of our calamitous fall from grace. We might well do all this if the man overboard in question is our mortal enemy, aware that by the time we were through with our analysis he would be food for the fishes. Otherwise, however, we are unlikely to scratch our heads over what on earth these words could mean. Their meaning is made apparent by their environment. This would still be the case even if the cry was a hoax. If we were not at sea the cry might make no sense, but hearing the chugging of the ship's engines settles the matter definitively.

In most practical settings, we do not have much of a choice over meaning. It tends to be determined by the setting itself. Or at least, the situation narrows down the range of possible meanings to a manageable few. When I see an exit sign over the door of a department store, I know from the context that it means 'This is the way out when you want to leave', not 'Leave now!' Otherwise such stores would be permanently empty. The word is descriptive rather than imperative. I take the instruction 'One tablet to be taken three times daily' on my bottle of aspirin to be addressed to me, not to all two hundred people in my apartment block. A driver who flashes his lights may mean either 'Watch it!' or 'Come on!', but this potentially fatal ambiguity results in fewer road accidents than one might expect, since the meaning is usually clear from the situation.

The problem with a poem or story, however, is that it does not arrive as part of a practical context. It is true that we know from words such as 'poem', 'novel', 'epic', 'comedy' and so on what sort of thing to expect, just as the way a literary work is packaged, advertised, marketed and reviewed plays an important part in determining our response to it. Beyond these vital signals, however, the work does not come to us with much of a setting at all. Instead, it creates its own setting as it goes along. We have to figure out from what it says a background against which what it says will make some sense. In fact, we are continually constructing such interpretative frames as we read, for the most part unconsciously. When we read Shakespeare's line 'Farewell! Thou art too dear for my possessing,' we think to ourselves, 'Ah, he's probably talking to his lover, and it looks as though they're breaking up. Too dear for his possessing, eh? Maybe she's been a bit too free with his money.' But there is nothing beyond the words themselves to inform us of this, as there is something beyond a cry of 'Fire!' to tell us how to make sense of it. (The smouldering hair of the person doing the shouting, for example.) And this makes the business of determining a literary work's meaning rather more arduous.

If works of literature were simply historical reports, we might be able to decide what they meant by reconstructing the historical situations from which they arose. But they are clearly not. They have a looser relation to their original conditions than that. *Moby-Dick* is not a sociological treatise on the American whaling industry. The novel draws on that context to fashion an imaginative world, but the significance of that world is not confined to it. This is not necessarily to suggest that the book is detached from its historical situation in a way that makes it universal in its appeal. There may well be civilisations that would not get much out of it. Some group of people in the distant future might find it incomprehensible, or tedious in the extreme. They might consider that having your leg chewed off by an enormous white whale is unbelievably boring, and thus not fit material for fiction. Could a future civilisation also find Horace's odes or Montaigne's essays tedious and unintelligible? Perhaps that future has already arrived, to some extent at least.

We do not know whether Melville's work is of universal interest because we have not reached the end of history yet, despite the best efforts of some of our political leaders. Nor have we consulted the Dinka or Tuareg on the matter. We do know, however, that calling *Moby-Dick* a novel means among other things that it is intended to say something about what we might broadly call 'moral' issues. I mean by this not ethical codes or religious prohibitions, but questions of human feelings, actions and ideas. *Moby-Dick* is trying to tell us something about guilt, evil, desire and psychosis, not just about blubber and harpoons, and not just something about nineteenth-century America.

This, in fact, is one thing we mean by the word 'fiction'. Fiction does not primarily mean a piece of writing which is not true. Truman Capote's *In Cold Blood*, Norman Mailer's *The Executioner's Song* and Frank McCourt's *Angela's Ashes* are all offered to us as true, yet they translate the truths they convey into a kind of imaginative fiction. Works of fiction can be full of factual information. You could even run a farm on the basis of what Virgil's *Georgics* has to say about agriculture, though it is doubtful that it would survive for very long. Yet texts we call literary are not written primarily to give us facts. Instead, the reader is invited to 'imagine' those facts, in the sense of constructing an imaginary world out of them. A work can thus be true and imagined, factual and fictional, at the same time. It belongs to the fictional world of Dickens's *A Tale of Two Cities* that you have to cross a stretch of sea to get from London to Paris, but this is also a fact. It is as though this fact is 'fictionalised' by the novel. It is put to work in a context in which its truth or falsehood is not the main point. What matters is how it behaves within the imaginative logic of the work. There is a difference between being true to the facts and being true to life. To say that there is a lot of truth in *Hamlet* does not mean that there really was a Danish prince who was either mad, pretending to be mad or both, and who treated his girlfriend abominably.

Works of fiction may tell us that Dallas is not in the same country as St Petersburg, or that an oculus is the central boss of a volute. They may make reference to facts with which almost everybody is wearily familiar, telling us for the umpteenth time that a seton is a skein of absorbent material passed below the skin and left with the ends protruding in order to promote the drainage of fluid or to act as a counter-irritant. What makes such works fictional is that these facts are not provided for their own sake, as they might be in a medical textbook, or for any practical purpose. They are used to help build up a certain way of seeing. Works of fiction are thus allowed to bend the facts to suit this purpose. They are more like politicians' speeches than the weather forecast. When they falsify bits of reality, we assume they are doing so for artistic reasons. If a writer consistently spells 'Buckingham', as in the royal palace, with a capital F, we would probably assume that she is making some sort of political point, not that she is illiterate. We do not charge an author with unpardonable ignorance because his twelfth-century characters never stop arguing about The Smiths. It is possible that the writer, having only a feeble grasp of history, really does believe that The Smiths were around in the twelfth century, or that Morrissey is such a superlative genius as to be timeless. But the fact that this occurs in a work of fiction inclines us to the charitable view that the distortion is deliberate. This is highly convenient for poets and novelists. Literature, like an absolute monarch among his fawning courtiers, is where you can never be wrong.

A realist novel presents characters and events which seem to exist independently of itself. We know, however, that this is an illusion, and that the work is actually fashioning this world as it goes along. This is one reason why some theorists hold that works of literature only ever refer to themselves. There never was an Ahab or Joe Christmas. Even if we discovered that there is a real-life Harry Potter, and that he is currently a registered heroin addict living in an Amsterdam squat, it would make no difference to our reading of the novels. It could be that there actually was a detective called Sherlock Holmes, and that unknown to Conan Doyle all the events recorded in the Holmes stories actually happened to him down to the last detail. Yet the stories would still not be about him. They would still be fictional.

Fictionality is one reason why literary works tend to be more ambiguous than non-literary ones. Because they lack practical contexts we have fewer clues to determine what they mean, so that phrases, events or characters can lend themselves to different readings. Or it may simply be that writers find themselves lapsing unconsciously into ambiguity, or do so deliberately to enrich their works. Among such ambiguities are sexual double entendres. One of Shakespeare's sonnets opens with the lines 'When my love swears that she is made of truth, / I do believe her, though I know she lies.' Alongside its obvious meaning, this could also mean 'When my love swears that she is indeed a virgin (maid, of truth), I do believe her, though I know she has sexual intercourse (lies).' In Richardson's *Clarissa*, we are told that the sexually voracious Lovelace, who is also a great scribbler of letters, 'has always a pen in his fingers when he retires'. Richardson is surely aware of the double meaning. The same is true of Dickens in *Nicholas Nickleby*, a novel which at one point shows us the demure Mary Graham sitting beside her beloved Tom Pinch at his organ in a rural church: 'She touched his organ, and from that happy epoch even it, the old companion of his happiest hours, incapable as he had thought it of elevation, began a new and deified existence.' Only the charitable or naive will imagine that this ambiguity is unintended. When Jane Eyre notes with quiet satisfaction how round and supple Mr Rochester's hand is, her words may have a less innocent implication, though one which is probably unconscious. This is unlikely to be true of the fact that one of Henry James's characters is called Fanny Assingham.

Some works of literature are more resistant to interpretation than others. As civilisation grows more complex and fragmentary, so does human experience, and so too does its literary medium, which is language. The later fiction of Henry James is so stylistically convoluted that he was once described as chewing more than he could bite off. A whole critical essay has been written on the first paragraph of his novel *The Ambassadors*, seeking valiantly to make sense of what on earth is going on. The following passage from *The Wings of the Dove* is by no means the most tortuous example of his later style:

> It was not moreover by any means with not having the imagination of expenditure that she appeared to charge her friend, but with not having the imagination of terror, of thrift, the imagination or in any degree the habit of a conscious dependence on others. Such moments, when all Wigmore Street, for instance, seemed to rustle about and the pale girl herself to be facing the different rustlers, usually so undiscriminated, as individual Britons too, Britons personal, parties to a relation and perhaps even intrinsically remarkable – such moments in especial determined for Kate a perception of the high happiness of her companion's liberty.

It is a far cry from Dan Brown. Like a lot of modernist writing, James's prose refuses to slip down easily. It poses a challenge to a culture of instant consumption. Instead, the reader is forced into a sweated labour of decipherment. It is as though reader and author become co-creators of the work, as the reader is drawn into the twists and turns of the syntax in a struggle to unpack the author's meaning. James feels the need to spin his syntax into a spider's web in order to catch every nuance of experience and every flicker of consciousness.

This super-subtlety is one of several reasons why modernist works of art can be obscure, and thus hard to interpret. Marcel Proust, whose prose is rarely less than lucid, can nevertheless produce sentences which stretch for half a page, full of labyrinthine alleys and syntactical byways, propelling the meaning of a passage around any number of tight grammatical corners and hairpin bends. *Ulysses* ends with an unpunctuated sentence which goes on not for half a page but for sixty or so pages, liberally spattered with obscenities. It is as though the opaqueness and complexity of modern existence are beginning to infiltrate the very form of literary works, not just their content.

The contrast with realist fiction is clear. In a lot of realist writing, language is made to seem as transparent as possible, yielding up its meaning without much resistance. It thus creates the effect of presenting reality in the raw. We may compare the James extract in this respect with a typical passage from Daniel Defoe's *Moll Flanders*:

It was near five weeks that I kept my bed, and tho' the violence of my feaver abated in three weeks, yet it several times return'd; and the physicians said two or three times, they could do no more for me, but that they must leave Nature and the distemper to fight it out; only strengthening the first with cordials to maintain the struggle: After the end of five weeks I grew better, but was so weak, so alter'd, so melancholly, and recover'd so slowly, that the physicians apprehended I should go into a consumption . . .

Language like this lacks all thickness and texture. It is used purely as an instrument. There is no sense of it being valued as a medium in itself. Defoe's prose is eminently consumable, drawing not the slightest attention to itself. James's style, by contrast, rubs our noses in the fact that whatever happens in a work of literature happens in terms of language. Tempestuous break-ups and tragic breakdowns are just a set of black marks. From time to time, such language may modestly efface itself, as it does in Defoe. By making itself unobtrusive, it may create the effect of giving us direct access to what it deals with. It may appear to dispense with artifice or convention. Yet this is an illusion. The Defoe passage is no 'closer to reality' than the passage from James. No piece of language is closer to reality than any other. The relationship between language and reality is not a spatial one. It is also true that Defoe's prose works just as much by conventions as, say, Milton's *Lycidas*. It is simply that we are more familiar with these conventions, and thus fail to notice them.

While we are on the topic of realism, we might note an important point about it. When we describe a work as realist, we do not mean that it is closer to reality in some absolute way than non-realist literature. We mean that it conforms to what people of a certain time and place tend to regard as reality. Imagine that we were to stumble upon a piece of writing from some ancient culture which seemed curiously preoccupied with the length of its characters' shinbones. We might conclude that this was some outlandishly avant-garde flight of fancy. Then we might come across a historical account of the same culture and realise that length of shinbone was what determined your place in the social pecking order. Those with long shinbones were banished to the desert and forced to eat dung, while those with the minimum of distance between knee and ankle stood an excellent chance of being elected king. In which case, we would be forced to reclassify the text as realist.

A visitor from Alpha Centauri who was handed a history of humanity, complete with wars, famines, genocides and massacres, might suppose that this was some outrageously surrealist text. There is a great deal in human history that beggars belief. Awarding the Nobel Peace Prize to a politician who illegally bombed Cambodia is merely one example. For psychoanalytic thought, dreams and fantasies bring us closer to the truth about ourselves than our waking life. Yet if these dreams and fantasies were to be put in fictional form, we would probably not regard the result as a realist work. In any case, there are very few purely realist works. A lot of supposedly realist texts contain some grossly improbable features. In Conrad's *Heart of Darkness*, we are told that a woman's face 'had a tragic and fierce aspect of wild sorrow and of dumb pain mingled with the fear of some struggling, half-shaped resolve'. This impossible facial expression exists only at the level of language. It is doubtful that even the most talented of actors could look tragic, fierce, wild, sorrowful, pained, fearful and half resolved at the same time. An Oscar would be a poor reward for such a performance.

If Joyce's *Finnegans Wake* rebuffs interpretation, it is partly because it is written in a number of different languages at the same time. Joyce's compatriot J.M. Synge was said to be the only man who could write in English and Irish simultaneously. Like all of Joyce's writing, the *Wake* reveals a profound trust in the power of the word, but this is not true of modernism in general. Modernism sends words out on a spree, but this is not generally because it has a robust faith in them. It is more typical of it to be distrustful of language, as with T.S. Eliot and Samuel Beckett. Can it really capture the immediacy of human experience, or allow us a glimpse of absolute truth? If it is to do so, it must be thickened and dislocated, made more intricate and allusive; and this is one reason why some modernist works are so hard to decipher. Language in its everyday state is shop-soiled and inauthentic, and only by doing violence to it can it become supple enough to reflect our experience. It is from this period that we inherit the high-sounding clichés that reflect so many twentieth-century attitudes to language: 'there's a breakdown of communication', 'words are just so inadequate', 'silence is so much more eloquent than speech', 'if I could tell you I would let you know'. In modern cinema, not least in France, phrases like these are spoken by two people in bed staring soulfully into each other's eyes, punctuated by unbearably long silences.

\* \* \*

We can now turn to some of the interpretative issues I raised at the start of the book. Let us take the following well-known literary text:

*Baa baa black sheep,*
*Have you any wool?*
*Yes, sir, yes, sir,*
*Three bags full.*

*One for the master*
*And one for the dame,*
*And one for the little boy*
*Who lives down the lane.*

This, to be sure, is not the most subtle piece of literature ever penned. There have been more searching investigations of the human condition. Even so, the verse raises a number of intriguing questions. To begin with, who speaks the first line? Is it an omniscient narrator, or a character with whom the sheep is in dialogue? And why does he say 'Baa baa black sheep, have you any wool?', instead of, say, 'Excuse me, Mr (or Ms) black sheep, have you any wool?' Is the speaker's query a purely academic one? Does he want to know how much wool the sheep has simply out of idle curiosity, or is there a less disinterested motive at work here?

It is a fair conjecture that the speaker asks the question because he wants some of the wool for himself. In that case, however, his mode of addressing the animal ('Baa baa black sheep') seems distinctly odd. It is possible that Baa baa is the sheep's name, and that the speaker of the verse is simply being polite. Perhaps he is being polite because he wants something from the creature. 'Baa baa black sheep' may be the same kind of construction as 'Henry black sheep', or 'Emily black sheep' (the animal's gender is indeterminate). But this is surely implausible. Baa baa is a strange name for a sheep. It sounds less like the beast's name than the noise it makes. (Though there are problems of translation here. Japanese or Korean sheep almost certainly do not say 'baa baa'. Perhaps sheep which belong to the Queen speak with a rather more upper-class accent and say 'bahr bahr'.)

Could it be that the speaker is actually imitating the animal to its face, making a satirical bleating sound in the act of addressing it, as one might say 'Moo moo, cow' or 'Bow wow, doggie'? If this is the case, it is surely an astonishingly tactless thing to do. Mocking someone's way of speaking is scarcely the most foolproof way of getting something out of them. This speaker, then, is not only ill mannered; he is also remarkably obtuse. He does not see that insulting the sheep to its face is blatantly not in his interests. He is clearly something of a sheepist, with an odiously superior attitude to our ovine colleagues. Perhaps he has fallen victim to a vulgar stereotype, assuming that sheep are too stupid to mind being sent up in this way.

If so, he has evidently miscalculated. For the insult does not pass unnoticed. 'Yes,' replies the sheep, 'I do indeed have some wool – three full bags of it, in fact. That's one for the master, one for the dame, and one for the little boy who lives down the lane. But none for you, you impudent bastard.' The last words, of course, are merely implied. To pronounce them openly would be to undermine the sheep's cleverly calculated pose of genial co-operation. He answers the speaker's question readily and at some length, but not at all in a way that the questioner is likely to find gratifying. Part of what the beast does, in fact, is deliberately misunderstand the question as an academic one. He cunningly refuses to pick up the speaker's implied meaning ('May I have some wool?'). It is as though one were to ask someone in the street 'Do you have the time?', and he were to reply 'Sure' and walk on. He has answered your question but failed to draw the correct inference from it.

In this sense, the poem illustrates a vital aspect of human meaning, namely the role played by inference and implication. To ask your guest 'Would you care for a cup of coffee?' is to indicate your readiness to give her one. Imagine being asked this by someone and then finding, when the coffee failed to appear, that it was merely an academic enquiry, along the lines of 'How many seamstresses were there in sixteenth-century Wales?' or 'How are you doing?' 'How are you doing?' is not an invitation to recount your recent medical history in grisly detail.

An alternative version of the poem reads 'But none for the little boy who lives down the lane'. (Those with an interest in cultural difference might note that there are also alternative ways of singing it. The British version differs slightly from the American.) Perhaps the little boy who lives down the lane is the speaker himself, and this is a sardonically roundabout way of letting him know that there is no wool for him. The refusal is sadistically reinforced by the fact that the sheep has just told us that there are three bags available, and thus in principle one for the little boy. Maybe the sheep is familiar with the speaker's name but frostily refuses to use it in retaliation for the abusive 'Baa baa'. Or perhaps the little boy is not identical with the questioner, in which case it is puzzling that the sheep should mention him. It seems to be a little more information than is strictly necessary. The sheep may simply be demonstrating his power to grant or withhold wool as he pleases, as an ominous warning to his interrogator. It may be his way of regaining the upper hand after the opening put-down. There is clearly a power-struggle afoot here.

What is wrong with this analysis, apart from its gross improbability? Obviously the fact that it looks only at content and not at form. We also need to note the leanness and economy of the verse, the way it sets its face against any verbal exuberance or excess. All the words of the poem except three are monosyllables. The language, which is image-free, aims in realist style for a transparency of word to thing. The metrical scheme is tight – more so, in fact, than the rhyming pattern, which contains a half-rhyme or para-rhyme ('dame' and 'lane'). You can read each line of the verse as having two stressed syllables (though this is not the only way of scanning it), which restricts what the speaking voice can make of it. By contrast, an iambic pentameter like 'Shall I compare thee to a summer's day?' is flexible enough to be voiced in a whole variety of ways. An actor can choose within reason where to lay the stresses, just as he or she can choose what pace, pitch, volume and intonation to go for. The five stresses of the metre (Shall *I* com*pare* thee *to* a *sum*mer's *day*?) provide a stable background against which the improvisations of the speaking voice can be played off. An actor who delivered the line with the stresses as I have just marked them would be unlikely to receive a standing ovation.

The metrical scheme of 'Baa baa black sheep', by contrast, determines the way the line is voiced rather more rigorously. It leaves less room for 'personality' in the speaker. It is a bit like the contrast between set dancing and the way you gyrate in a night club. Because the stresses of the verse are so regular and emphatic, it sounds more like a chant or ritual than a piece of conversation. Even so, you could use tone to convey the kind of interpretation I have just sketched. You could begin with a sardonic cackle ('Baa baa'), follow it up with a curt, imperious 'Have you any wool?', and then have the sheep speak its lines in an elaborately mock-courteous way, with mutedly aggressive undertones.

Part of the poem's effect lies in the contrast between its form and its content. The form is simple and artless – a childlike chant which slims language down to a set of brief notations. Its lucidity suggests a world in which things are unambiguous and out in the open. Yet this is hardly confirmed by the poem's content, as we have just seen. Its transparent surface conceals a whole set of conflicts, tensions, manipulations and misunderstandings. These characters may not quite be out of the late Henry James, but their discourse is awash with ambiguities and insinuations. Beneath the text itself lies a complex subtext of power, malice, domination and false deference. Few works could be more profoundly political. 'Baa Baa Black Sheep' makes Marx's *Capital* look like *Mary Poppins*.

Would anyone think this was true? It is hard to imagine so. The reading of the piece I have just offered would seem too ridiculous even to consider. Quite apart from its fancifulness, it overlooks the question of genre. The nursery rhyme is a specific genre or type of literature, and like any genre it has its peculiar rules and conventions. One of these is that such verses are not supposed to mean very much. It is a mistake to treat them as though they were Goethe's *Faust* or Rilke's *Sonnets to Orpheus*. They are ritualised songs, not diagnoses of the human condition. Nursery rhymes are communal chants, flights of fancy and forms of verbal play. They sometimes consist of a collection of images which seem fairly random, and are not expected to display much narrative coherence. There is something oddly inconsequential about their storylines (think of 'Little Miss Muffet', 'Sing a Song of Sixpence' or 'Goosey Goosey Gander'), as though they are half-remembered fragments of longer narratives that have been lost in the mists of time. 'Hey Diddle Diddle, the Cat and the Fiddle' is an Eliotic cluster of cryptic images which refuse to form a unified narrative. To read these rhymes as though they were *Bleak House* or *The Duchess of Malfi* is as much a mistake as to measure Paul McCartney against Mozart. They are simply distinct modes. Verses of this kind are full of minor puzzles and obscure allusions. 'Humpty Dumpty', for example, seems to think it worth mentioning that the king's horses failed to reassemble an egg, even though no horse on historical record has been known to do that.

All this, however, does not settle the question of whether the verse can be read in the way I have proposed. This, let us note, is not the same as asking whether it was composed to be read in this way. Almost certainly not. Even so, you can choose to interpret a piece of writing in ways it plainly did not or could not anticipate. There may be some seriously strange types who find manuals for assembling table lamps hauntingly poetic in their descriptions of plugs and flexes, and who read them avidly far into the night. Such manuals might even have proved cause for divorce. Yet it is unlikely that whoever wrote them would have anticipated such a use. The question, then, is why 'Baa Baa Black Sheep' cannot mean what I have suggested it means. Why is this reading illicit, if indeed it is?

We cannot, of course, appeal to the author's meaning here, because we have no idea who the author was. Even if we did, it would not necessarily settle the question. Authors can offer accounts of their own works which sound even more absurd than the one I have just provided for 'Baa Baa Black Sheep'. T.S. Eliot, for example, once described *The Waste Land* as no more than a piece of rhythmical grousing. The only problem with this comment is that it is palpably untrue. Thomas Hardy quite often disclaimed having any views at all about the controversial subjects presented in his fiction. When asked what one of his more obscure poems meant, Robert Browning is said to have replied, 'When I wrote this poem, God and Robert Browning knew what it meant. Now, God knows.' If Sylvia Plath were to have confided that her poetry was really about collecting antique clocks, we would probably be forced to conclude that she was mistaken. There are writers who consider their work to be examples of high seriousness when they are hilariously, unintentionally funny. We shall be considering such an author at the very end of the book. Another example is the Book of Jonah, which is probably not intended to be funny but which is brilliantly comic without seeming to be aware of it.

## Interpretation

Authors may have long forgotten what they intended a poem or story to mean. In any case, works of literature do not mean just one thing. They are capable of generating whole repertoires of meaning, some of which alter as history itself changes, and not all of which may be consciously intended. Much of what I had to say of literary texts in the first chapter would no doubt have come as news to their creators. Flann O'Brien probably did not realise that the opening paragraph of *The Third Policeman* could be read as implying that John Divney was thick-headed enough to spend his time turning an iron bar into a bicycle-pump with the specific intention of killing old Mathers with it. E.M. Forster may well have been surprised to learn that the first four phrases of *A Passage to India* have roughly three stresses each. It is unlikely that Robert Lowell could have provided a detailed account of how the metre and the syntax work athwart each other in the opening lines of 'The Quaker Graveyard in Nantucket'. When Yeats writes of a 'terrible beauty' in his poem 'Easter 1916', the phrase may well refer to his beloved Maud Gonne as well as to the military uprising in Dublin, but he was probably oblivious of the fact.

Behind the belief that the author is the key to a work's meaning lies a particular conception of literature. This is the doctrine of literature as self-expression, much favoured by some creative writing courses. On this theory, a literary work is the sincere expression of some experience that the author has had, and which he wishes to share with others. This is a fairly recent idea, dating mostly from romanticism. It would no doubt have come as a surprise to Homer, Dante and Chaucer. Alexander Pope would have found it puzzling, while Ezra Pound and T.S. Eliot would have scornfully dismissed it. It is not clear what personal experience the author of the *Iliad* was trying to share with us.

There are certain obvious ways in which the idea of literature as self-expression is flawed, not least when it is taken too literally. Shakespeare, as far as we know, was never marooned on a magical island, but *The Tempest* has an authentic ring to it even so. Even if he did spend time eating coconuts and knocking a raft together, it would not necessarily have made his last work a finer play. The novelist Lawrence Durrell spent some time in Alexandria, but some readers of his *Alexandria Quartet* would rather he had not. When Shakespeare writes of his lover in his sonnets, it may be that he never had a lover at all. No doubt it made a difference to him whether he had or not, but it does not make a difference to us.

One should not make a fetish of personal experience. Aspiring writers are sometimes advised to draw on their own experience, but how could they not? They can only write of what they are aware of, and awareness is as much part of one's experience as a tap on the skull. Sophocles writes out of his own experience in *Oedipus the King*, though it is unlikely that he was a blind, exiled, incestuous parricide. You can have experience of gluttony without being a glutton yourself. You can grasp the concept of gluttony, discuss the idea with others, read tales of gluttons exploding all over the walls after devouring one pork pie too many and so on. There is no reason why a celibate could not come up with a more sensitive portrayal of human sexuality than a thrice-married roué.

A writer may not experience anything beyond the experience of the act of writing. Perhaps the agonised feelings he records are entirely fictional. He may never have had a tortoise called John Henry Newman, or have wandered dazed and bleeding around the alleyways of Tangiers. Or perhaps he staggers bleeding around Tangiers every three days, but writes about it in so unconvincing a way that we suspect he does not. There is not much point in trying to peer behind a poem to see whether the poet really felt as he says he did, unless he is declaring his passion for his secretary and you happen to be his wife. The experience of a poem is not best thought of as something 'behind' it, which the poet then struggles to convey into language. What is the experience 'behind' the words 'Thou still unravished bride of quietness'? And can we identify it without simply repeating the words? Language in poetry is a reality in itself, not simply a vehicle for something distinct from it. The experience which matters is the experience of the poem itself. The relevant feelings and ideas are those which are bound up with the words themselves, not something separable from them. Bad actors ruin good poetry by foisting their feelings upon it in lavish emotional displays, not realising that the feelings are in some sense present in the language itself.

Surely, though, an author must be sincere? Sincerity, as it happens, is not a concept that makes much sense in critical discussion. Nor does it sometimes make much sense in real life. We do not justify Attila the Hun by pointing to the fact that he was sincere in what he did. What would it mean to say that Jane Austen was sincere in portraying the odious Mr Collins, or that Alexander Pope was being sincere when he wrote 'For fools rush in where angels fear to tread'? We can speak of pieces of language as being vacuous or visceral, bombastic or intensely moving, histrionic or shot through with loathing. But this is not the same as talking about an author in these terms. A writer may strive to be sincere yet end up producing a bogus-sounding piece of art. One could not be burningly sincere in words which were absurd or completely empty. I could not say 'I love you as I love a cornflake spinning on its nose in the armpit of an isosceles triangle' and passionately mean it. There is nothing there to mean, passionately or not. It would be kinder to get me to a doctor than to a registry office.

Is Samuel Beckett being sincere when he portrays humanity in such bleak terms? Is this a matter of self-expression on his part? Isn't it possible that the real-life Beckett was a jovial, dewy-eyed soul who looked forward to the imminent arrival of an earthly paradise? As a matter of fact, we know that he was not. The real-life Beckett was in some ways a fairly morose character, even though he enjoyed a drink, a joke and a spot of congenial company. But it is not out of the question that he regularly had his friends rolling on the floor clutching their sides and howling for him to stop. He might also have believed that humankind was destined for a gloriously fulfilling future. Perhaps his work is simply an experiment in seeing the world as a post-nuclear landscape. Or perhaps adopting this attitude provisionally was the most effective way he could write. Shakespeare could create some compellingly nihilistic characters (Iago, for example, or the psychopathic Barnadine in *Measure for Measure*) without being a nihilist himself. Or at least not as far as we know.

To doubt whether an author can be fully in command of his or her meanings is not to suggest that literary works can mean anything you like. If we were to read 'Baa Baa Black Sheep' as an account of the electrification of the early Soviet Union, it would be hard to see a relation between this account of it and the text itself, so that there would be a logical problem about how it could count as a reading of this particular work. There might seem no reason why it could not serve as an interpretation of any literary work at all. Maybe Stalin thought *Paradise Lost* was also about the electrification of the early Soviet Union. In a similar way, 'Enormous, flapping, puce-coloured ears' is not just an eccentric answer to the question 'How old are you?' It is no answer at all. There seems to be no connection between the two utterances. To claim that Yeats's phrase 'terrible beauty' may refer among other things to Maud Gonne is not sheer speculation, like arguing that Virginia Woolf's lighthouse is a symbol of the Indian Mutiny. We can read the figure of Maud Gonne into the words 'terrible beauty' because we know something of what she meant for Yeats, what ambiguities and symbolic resonances she evoked for him, how he depicts her in his other poems and so on. Critics have to be able to back up their claims.

Which returns us to the question of why this version of 'Baa Baa Black Sheep' may be invalid. How does one reply to someone who exclaims 'But it obviously can't mean that!' One retort is to point out that I have just shown that it can. I have argued the case line by line, adducing evidence for my claims and demonstrating how the reading is coherent. Why is the phrase 'Baa baa' *obviously* not a satirical bleat by the narrator? Where is the evidence to say so? Who says that he doesn't have an avaricious eye on the sheep's wool?

Where, however, is the evidence to say he does? It is true that the poem does not actually state that the narrator is being boorish and overbearing, or that the sheep is craftily trying to get even with him. But literary texts often work by unspoken implications. In fact, every utterance in the world depends on a whole host of such implications – so many, in fact, that we would never be able to explicate them all. To say 'Put the garbage out' is usually taken to refer to one's own garbage. There is no suggestion that one should make a complicated, expensive trek to Hollywood in order to put Jack Nicholson's garbage out for him, even if the statement does not actually rule it out. *The Turn of the Screw* does not tell us that its narrator is psychotic, but this is a reasonable implication to read into it. We are not told by Graham Greene's *Brighton Rock* that Pinkie, its black-hearted protagonist, is en route to hell, but the novel would make a lot less sense if this were not true. We assume that Lear has two legs, two lungs and a liver, but the play does not mention those facts. The problem is one of what counts as a reasonable inference in a specific situation. And this is a matter of judgement, which cannot be reduced to rules. It is something we simply have to argue about.

I have already conceded that my account of 'Baa Baa Black Sheep' is almost certainly not what its anonymous author meant by it. Or, for that matter, what the children who sing it today imagine that it means. My case is simply that the verses can be construed in this way without sidelining some vital textual evidence, running headlong into logical contradiction, or finding implications in the lines which could not possibly be present. If, for example, one was intent on trying to respect the original meaning as far as possible, 'Baa baa' could not be taken as referring to the sound of a motor-bike starting up, since the rhyme long predates such machines. If a reading of the piece depended on the little boy who lives down the lane being the narrator himself, it would be seriously undermined if there turned out to be a convention by which the phrase 'the little boy who lives down the lane', when used in nursery rhymes, always refers to the person who speaks it, rather as the phrase 'Son of Man' in the New Testament is among other things a conventional way of referring to oneself in Aramaic. The sheep would then be giving wool to himself, or (in another version of the piece) refusing to. But there is no such convention.

So it is not that there is enough textual evidence to work against this version of the poem. It is rather that there is not enough evidence to support it. This is why the reading seems fanciful and far-fetched. It is possible, but not persuasive. It depends a fair amount on tone, and since tone cannot literally be heard in literature, it can often prove a source of ambiguity. A change of tone can signal a shift of meaning. The reading probably finds more in the text than the text can reasonably support, though not more than it can *logically* support.

To say that my construal of the poem is unconvincing is to say that it offends the sense that we habitually make of things, a fact that is not to be swept aside. It is a piece of intellectual arrogance to sweep aside the tacit agreements and assumptions embedded in everyday life. They can often distil a good deal of wisdom. Yet common sense is not always to be trusted. Racial equality was offensive to common sense in 1960s Alabama. As for fanciful interpretations, it has been seriously argued that 'Goosey Goosey Gander' is about the raiding of the homes of recusant Roman Catholic noblemen by Cromwell's troops during the seventeenth-century civil war in England. 'Goosey' refers to the goose-stepping gait of the soldiers as they break into the bedchamber of a Catholic noblewoman, while the old man who is thrown downstairs for not saying his prayers is a Catholic chaplain who refuses to bow to the new Protestant forms of worship. This may well be true. Superficially, however, it seems just as implausible as my account of 'Baa Baa Black Sheep'.

There is another point to be noted. 'Goosey Goosey Gander' may originally have been about religious strife in seventeenth-century England, but it is not about this for the children who sing it in the school playground today. For them, it is simply about a man wandering upstairs into his wife's bedroom. Does this mean that their version of the rhyme is unacceptable? Not at all. It is just that what it means to them is not what it may have meant a few centuries ago. But this is true of many works of literature. Nor can the original meaning, assuming that we have access to it, always pull rank over what the piece may come to signify later. It may be that in some ways we can understand a work of the past better than its contemporaries could. Modern psychoanalytic insights, for example, might make more sense of William Blake's 'Songs of Experience' than the kind of knowledge available at the time. The experience of twentieth-century despotism might enrich our understanding of Shakespeare's *Julius Caesar*. It is unlikely that the figure of Shylock in *The Merchant of Venice* meant quite the same before the Holocaust as it does after it. If Richardson's *Clarissa* has become freshly 'readable' again in our time, after its contemptuous dismissal in the nineteenth century, it is partly on account of the modern women's movement. There is a sense in which we know more about the past than the past did because we know what it led to. In any case, living through a historical event is not the same as understanding it. All the same, there are forms of historical knowledge which are simply lost to us. Perhaps we will never know for sure what the people who flocked to see *Hamlet* when it was first staged thought about the morality of revenge, assuming that they knew themselves.

Imagine that it was a convention of the nursery rhyme genre that one should always search the work for occult meanings. Something like this is true of the Kabbalistic tradition of biblical interpretation. One might be required to assume that there is an endless fund of abstruse meanings in the text waiting to be dug out. Alternatively, there might be a recommendation to read them in. It might be part of the meaning of a nursery rhyme, rather like a Rorschach blot, that you were allowed to make your own subjective sense of it. Or it might be that you were invited to make your own sense of it provided that the sense was logically coherent and seemed to fit with the textual evidence.

If this were so, then my version of 'Baa Baa Black Sheep' would no doubt be judged admissible. It is not an obviously valid reading. Its correctness does not exactly cry out from the house tops. Yet on such a theory of interpretation, it cannot be ruled out. Besides, the rhyme may not mean this now, but it might always come to do so. My account of it might prove to be a self-fulfilling prophecy. If it catches on, which I am quietly confident it will, children who chant this verse in the school playground for generations to come will think spontaneously of rude narrators and duplicitous sheep as they do so. My place in history will then be secure.

In the ancient Jewish practice of *midrash* or scriptural interpretation, it was sometimes deemed acceptable to assign new, strikingly improbable meanings to the Bible. The word *midrash* means to seek or investigate, and holy scripture was regarded as semantically inexhaustible. It was able to confront each commentator with a different sense each time it was studied. The Torah or sacred Jewish scriptures was seen as incomplete, and each generation of interpreters had to help bring it to perfection. No one of them, however, would ever have the last word. Moreover, unless a piece of scripture could be brought to bear on the needs and preoccupations of its time, it was judged to be a dead letter. It had to be given life by being looked at in the light of the contemporary moment. You did not truly understand the text unless you found a way of putting it into practice.

My reading of 'Baa Baa Black Sheep', as it happens, is not of this kind. I am not doing anything as devious as appealing to *midrash* in order to justify it. It is not especially influenced by the needs and preoccupations of our time, other than in the sense that any act of reading is. It also claims to be true to the text as it stands, without doing flagrant interpretative violence to it. It is not, in other words, as daring or as radical as *midrash*. It does not argue that the black sheep is meant to be Bono, or that the three bags of wool stand for three reasons why neo-Keynesian theory is inapplicable to the modern Hungarian economy.

One reason why we might tolerate such apparently exotic accounts of texts is that when it comes to literature, not a lot is at stake. Nobody is going to lose their lives, or even their livelihoods, over the question of whether the narrator of 'Baa Baa Black Sheep' is surly and domineering, unless I teach this critical approach to students who report me to the Dean for professional incompetence and incurable frivolity. People may stand to lose their livelihoods, liberties or even lives, however, if a legal document is read in too free a way. Sometimes it is licence one wants and sometimes not, depending on what one might call the regime of reading in question. When it comes to roadsigns or medical prescriptions, a strictly literal, unambiguous meaning is desirable; at other times, as with jokes and modernist poems, playfulness and ambiguity may be the point. There are occasions when meaning needs at all costs to be nailed down, and other times when it may float triumphantly free. Some literary theorists would claim that if you happen to find this interpretation of 'Baa Baa Black Sheep' rewarding and thought-provoking, then that is enough reason to adopt it. Others would insist that such interpretations must be cognitive, in the sense of yielding us accurate knowledge of the work.

Literary works may best be seen not as texts with a fixed sense, but as matrices capable of generating a whole range of possible meanings. They do not so much contain meaning as produce it.

Once again, this is not to suggest that anything goes. There may be some conceivable situation in which 'Shall I compare thee to a summer's day?' could mean 'Just scratch a bit under the shoulder blade, will you?' Perhaps there is a tribe in the Amazon basin in whose language, by an amazing coincidence, the sounds of Shakespeare's line corresponds exactly to the sounds they make when they ask to be scratched a bit under the shoulder blade. Or perhaps some mighty cataclysm in the future will transform the English language so radically that when people murmur to us 'Shall I compare thee to a summer's day?', we instantly oblige by scratching their backs. For us and for now, however, that is not what Shakespeare's line signifies.

One reason for this is that meaning is a public affair. There could not be a meaning that only I was in possession of, as there could be a plot of land that only I owned. Meaning is not a matter of private property. I cannot privately decide to make the phrase 'hermeneutical phenomenology' mean 'Meryl Streep'. Meaning belongs to language, and language distils the sense we collectively make of our world. It is not free-floating. Rather, it is bound up with the ways we go to work on reality – with a society's values, traditions, assumptions, institutions and material conditions. In the end, we speak as we do because of the things that we do. To change a language decisively, you would have to change at least some of this. Meaning is not fixed in the sense that it is inherent in a specific set of words. If this were so, there could be no possibility of translation. If meaning is relatively determinate, it is because it is more than just a verbal affair. It signifies a compact between human beings in a specific place and time, embodying their shared ways of acting, feeling and perceiving. Even when people conflict over such things, they must agree to some extent on what it is they are arguing over, otherwise we could not call what they were doing conflicting. You and I cannot disagree over whether Sofia is hotter than Carolina if you think they are geographical locations and I think they are movie stars.

It follows from this that a work of literature could not mean something to me alone. I might see in it something that nobody else does, but what I see must in principle be sharable with others for us to call it a meaning. Indeed, I can only formulate a meaning to myself in language that I share with others. Perhaps the words 'black sheep' remind me irresistibly of Hugh Grant. Every time someone pronounces these words, an image of Hugh Grant flashes up spontaneously in my mind. This, however, could not be part of the meaning of the words. It is simply a random private association. Meaning is not objective in the sense that municipal cark parks are, but it is not just subjective either. The same is true of literary works themselves, as I have pointed out already. They are transactions, not material objects. There is no literature without a reader.

Moreover, a reader's ability to get a poem or novel to mean something is shaped by his or her historical situation. Here and now, a text can only mean whatever lies within a reader's capacity to make it mean. *Clarissa* could not shed light on feminist theory for its contemporary readership, but it can do for us. Readers bring all kinds of (often unconscious) beliefs and assumptions to a literary text. Among them will be a rough idea of what a literary work is in the first place, and some sense of what they are supposed to do with it. What they find in the text will be shaped by their beliefs and expectations, though it might also succeed in revolutionising them. Indeed, for some critics this is what makes for truly exceptional literary art. One might enter a poem an agnostic and emerge as a Jehovah's Witness.

# Interpretation

There is no single correct interpretation of 'Baa Baa Black Sheep', or for that matter of any other literary work. Even so, there are more and less plausible ways of making sense of it. A persuasive reading must take account of the textual evidence, though establishing this evidence itself involves interpretation. Someone might always protest 'I don't regard that as evidence!', or 'Where on earth do you get the idea that the *Macbeth* witches are meant to be evil?' Textual evidence can usually be construed in a variety of ways, and conflicts can arise between these versions. There may be no definitive way of deciding among them. Nor may we feel the need to do so. Could there be a convincing reading of a literary work that nobody has yet come up with, or that nobody ever will? Why not? Perhaps there are works which are standing by to be read in startlingly new ways, waiting to be brought to their full potential by some reader as yet unborn. Perhaps only the future will put us in firmer possession of the past.

\* \* \*

Unless a reader continually makes assumptions, a literary text will not work. Take, for example, the deliciously deadpan first sentence of Evelyn Waugh's short story 'Mr Loveday's Little Outing': ' "You will not find your father greatly changed," remarked Lady Moping, as the car turned into the gates of the County Asylum.' Like any piece of language, this sentence presents us with a number of blanks that we must fill in, however unconsciously, in order to make sense of it. In this sense, a fictional sentence is a bit like a scientific hypothesis. Like a hypothesis, we have to test it out in different ways until we find a way that works. We assume that the father to whom Lady Moping refers is her husband (though we have no evidence for this so far); that Lady Moping is visiting him in a lunatic asylum; and that she is bringing her child or children with her. Perhaps we also assume that the husband is a patient in the asylum, which makes the comment 'You will not find your father greatly changed' comic. It may mean, reassuringly, 'Don't worry, he's his usual self, every bit as normal as he was before he went in.' Or it may mean, rather less reassuringly, 'He's just as crazy as he was before they took him away.' It is the ambiguity which makes the remark funny, as well as the dry tone in which it is delivered. The fact that Lady Moping is predicting how her offspring will react to their father ('You will not find . . .') lends the statement the imperious ring of an instruction. Perhaps we suspect this to be typical of titled persons.

It is possible, however, Lady Moping's husband is not an inmate at all. He might be a nurse, a psychiatrist or a gardener. This, however, is rendered somewhat unlikely by the 'Lady'. Lady Moping is an aristocrat, her husband is probably Lord Moping, and noble lords do not generally become psychiatrists, let alone nurses or gardeners. There is, moreover, a general feeling that the English nobility are a little dotty, which reinforces the suspicion that Lord Moping is more likely to be a recipient of medical treatment than a dispenser of it. Besides, his child or children seem not to have seen him for some time, long enough anyway for him to have time to change, which might not be the case if he were a gardener or psychiatrist. The grammatical construction of the phrase 'as the car turned into the gates of the County Asylum' might suggest that Lady Moping herself is not driving, being rather too grand for such a menial activity. Perhaps she is sitting beside a chauffeur in the front of the car.

If readers bring assumptions to literary works, literary works can also intimate attitudes to their readers. A critic once described

Swift's stance to his readers as 'intimate but unfriendly'. There is a touch of good-humoured sadism about the way *Tristram Shandy* invites the reader to act as a kind of co-author, but in doing so forces him to work excessively hard to make sense of the text. A work may buttonhole the reader like an old crony, or maintain a formal, perhaps rather frosty attitude to her. It may strike up an unspoken pact with the reader, assuming that he is an erudite man of leisure who shares the same civilised values as itself. Or it may set out to disturb and disorientate those who pick it up, assaulting their senses, defamiliarising their convictions or violating their sense of decorum. There are also works which seem to turn their backs on an audience, communing with themselves in private while reluctantly allowing their meditations to be overheard.

\* \* \*

All knowledge depends to some extent on a process of abstraction. In the case of literary criticism, this means being able to stand back from the work and trying to see it in the round. This is not easy, partly because literary works are processes in time which are hard to see laid out as a whole. We also need to find a way of standing back which keeps us in touch with the work's tangible presence. One way in which we can try to grasp a poem or novel as a whole is by investigating its themes, meaning the pattern of preoccupations we find in it. In the analysis of Charles Dickens's novel *Great Expectations* that follows, this is one of the things I shall aim to do.

The most uninspired form of criticism simply tells the story of a work in different words. Some students imagine they are writing criticism when for the most part they are simply paraphrasing a text, occasionally throwing in the odd comment of their own. All the same, recounting what happens in a story or novel is sometimes unavoidable, so there follows a brief summary of Dickens's novel. Pip, the hero, lives as a child with his adult sister Mrs Joe and her childlike, kind-hearted husband Joe Gargery, who works as a blacksmith in the desolate marshlands of south-eastern England. Mrs Joe brings up Pip with a heavy hand, and inflicts something of the same harsh treatment on her long-suffering husband. Pip's parents are dead, and while inspecting their grave in the churchyard one day he is collared by a convict, Abel Magwitch, who has escaped from a nearby prison ship. Magwitch asks Pip for a file to free himself from his leg-iron, along with some food and drink, and the boy obliges by stealing these items from his home. But Magwitch is recaptured, and finds himself shipped off for life to the British penal colony in Australia.

Meanwhile, Pip is summoned by a rich, eccentric local gentlewoman, Miss Havisham, to her decaying home Satis House, where he is to play with her haughty, beautiful young ward Estella. Miss Havisham's life has been blighted by a lover who jilted her on their wedding day, and the clocks of Satis House have been halted at this fatal hour. She herself sits like a skeleton or ghastly waxwork amid the rotting, vermin-ridden remains of her wedding banquet, shrouded in her tattered wedding dress. Pip falls in love with Estella, whom Miss Havisham is bringing up with the express purpose of breaking men's hearts in revenge for her own ill-treatment. Unknown to him, young Pip has been brought along for Estella to limber up on.

As a result of his experience of Satis House, Pip becomes increasingly dissatisfied with his lowly existence at the forge, where he has been indentured as Joe's apprentice. He hatches ambitions to become a gentleman and by doing so to win Estella, who professes to despise his plebeian way of life. Meanwhile, Mrs Joe is savagely assaulted at the forge by the villainous Orlick, a labourer in Joe's employ, lingers on her sickbed for a while unable to speak, and finally dies. Joe then marries Biddy, a pleasant young schoolmistress less given to clipping him around the ear.

A London lawyer, Jaggers, arrives to inform Pip that an anonymous donor has bestowed a fortune upon him, and that he is to go to the capital to live as a gentleman. Pip, who assumes that his benefactor is Miss Havisham, and that she is grooming him to be a suitable partner for Estella, moves to the metropolis, and under the guardianship of the grim-faced Jaggers launches on a somewhat ungratifying life of leisure. He becomes a prig and a snob, disdainful of his previous life and odiously condescending to the injured but uncomplaining Joe. Even as a working-class child, he anticipates his future as a gentleman by speaking Standard English rather than the local accent. (So does Oliver Twist, who was brought up in a workhouse yet speaks like a chartered accountant. There was a general feeling in Victorian circles that heroes and heroines should not be allowed to drop their aitches or slur their vowels. The fact that the Artful Dodger speaks with a Cockney accent is not unrelated to the fact that he steals handkerchiefs.)

Magwitch then reappears abruptly on the scene, having escaped from his life in Australia, to inform Pip that it is he who is his secret benefactor. He has prospered while abroad, and made a gentleman out of the boy in gratitude for the help he gave him on the marshes. Pip receives this news with horror, and at first feels little but disgust for his new-found patron. Magwitch, who left Australia illegally, is being pursued by the authorities, and Pip arranges for him to be secretly shipped out of the country. Once again, however, the convict is arrested. He is sentenced to death, but dies before he can be hanged. Pip's feelings towards the felon have now softened, and he has learned that Magwitch, unknown to himself, is Estella's father. He tells the old man on his deathbed that he has a daughter whom he, Pip, dearly loves. In doing so, he grants the old lag a peaceful death.

Pip is now bitterly remorseful for his former snobbery and social ambition. Being no longer in possession of his fortune, he becomes a clerk and then a partner in a modest business enterprise. He has a grave illness, and is joyfully reunited with Joe and Biddy. Joe nurses him back to health like a baby, after which he encounters Estella once more. She, too, is now almost without possessions. Miss Havisham has died at a fire in her home, and before her death repents of the way she has set out to break Pip's heart. Estella, tempered by suffering like Pip himself, is equally humbled and contrite. She and Pip seem likely to marry, though Dickens's original ending was rather more sombre.

These, then, are the bare bones of the narrative, mercifully shorn of some outrageous coincidences and surreally improbable plotting. What significant patterns can we discover in it? We may note to begin with the extraordinary number of false parents that the story contains. Mrs Joe is Pip's sister but behaves as his mother, while her husband Joe Gargery is in the position of Pip's father but is in fact his best friend and metaphorical brother. In the end, to complicate matters further, Pip will recognise in Joe his true spiritual father. In this sense, the Gargery family is a grisly parody of a conventional one, with Mrs Joe acting as both sister and mother to Pip, and as both wife and mother to Joe. Joe, for his part, acts as both brother and father to Pip. One is reminded of Tom Lehrer's satirical song about Oedipus: 'He loved his mother like no other, / His daughter was his sister and his son was his brother.' Towards the end of the novel, Pip will nurse his spiritual father Magwitch as though he were a child. In doing so, he becomes, as one critic has put it, a father to his father. There is also a kind of sibling solidarity between the two men, since both were ill-used as children, just as there is between Pip and Joe. If the protagonist is to be redeemed, the criminal or negligent parent must be forgiven, as Cordelia pardons Lear, and the wayward child must accept forgiveness in his turn, in Pip's case from Joe and Biddy.

In its warmth and affection, the family in early Dickens often figures as a refuge from a harsh public world, which is true in this novel of the domestic set-up of Wemmick, Jaggers's good-hearted clerk. Yet turning the family into a safe haven is now so arduous a task that Wemmick's house actually has a moat around it, and can be entered only by a drawbridge. This Englishman's home is almost literally a castle. Public and domestic spheres are split apart. Only in this way can the latter be protected from the callousness of the former. Within the protective walls of the Wemmick household, there is abundant good feeling between Wemmick himself and his uproariously comic old father. Pip's family, by contrast, is morbidly dysfunctional, with mildly incestuous overtones. There is some deep sexual and domestic disturbance in the forge, as there is in Satis House. The word 'forge' means a blacksmith's workshop, but it also suggests fraudulence and deceit, which brings to mind both Satis House and Pip's status as a sham gentleman. Love and sexuality in Miss Havisham's diseased world are associated with violence, cruelty, power, fantasy and duplicity. Love in this novel is by no means a simple alternative to hatred and domination. It is intimately interwoven with them.

Pip's childhood home is physically attached to the forge, which means that, unlike Wemmick's mini-castle, the world of work over-laps with the domestic sphere. The negative aspect of this is that the violence and oppressiveness of the public world also infiltrate the private one. Joe's job as a blacksmith involves a good deal of hammering, and so does Mrs Joe's treatment of Pip. In fact, Joe tells the boy how his own father, a blacksmith averse to work, 'hammered at me with a wigour only to be equalled by the wigour with which he didn't hammer at his anwil'. Pip uses the word 'unjust' of Mrs Joe's belabouring of him, which links the violence of the domestic world to the public domain of law, crime and punishment. The forge is associated with iron, and it is with a piece of iron that Orlick strikes Mrs Joe down.

Yet this intimacy between work and home, public and private domains, is also to be prized. For better as well as for worse, there is a minimum of distance between the two realms in the Gargery household. Joe's qualities as a craftsman are related to his virtues as a friend and surrogate father. The later Dickens admires people who have practical skills rather than those who live off stocks and shares. Manual work is real, whereas paper wealth is parasitic on other people's labour. Magwitch's fortune was earned by the sweat of his brow, which is more than can be said of Miss Havisham's. So there is something authentic about the forge, just as there is something brittle and unreal about the world of wealth and privilege. In moving from his rural home to fashionable London, Pip is travelling from reality to illusion. He will finally have to reverse this journey if he is to be redeemed.

Miss Havisham is a substitute mother to the adopted Estella, while Magwitch is a substitute father to Pip. 'I'm your second father,' he tells Pip. 'You're my son – more to me than any son.' Since Magwitch is also Estella's literal father, we have another mild hint of incest here. Metaphorically speaking, Pip and Estella are brother and sister. In fact, it was because he believed his daughter to be dead that Magwitch 'adopted' Pip as a kind of compensation. Even Pip's remote relation Mr Pumblechook, an oily old humbug, takes a phoney paternal interest in him, while Jaggers, who is Pip's guardian, is yet another of his patrons. The kind-hearted Wemmick also gives him some fatherly care, while his friend Herbert Pocket teaches him how to conduct himself like a gentleman.

Some of these false parents are bad, while others are good. Mrs Joe and Miss Havisham are bad false parents, whereas Joe, Jaggers and Wemmick are good false ones. So is Magwitch, though more ambiguously so. But there are very few good true parents in the whole book. Miss Havisham is a wicked fairy godmother (she even has a crutch as a wand), while Magwitch is the good fairy who grants your wishes. It is, however, part of fairy lore that your yearnings rarely come true in the way you expect, which is certainly true in Pip's case. The magical fairy food can quickly turn to ashes in your mouth. Dreams of grandeur can veer into nightmare.

What are we to make of these bogus patriarchs, childlike adults, wicked stepmothers and semi-incestuous siblings? *Great Expectations* is preoccupied among other things with what we might call the question of origins. Where do we really come from? What are the true sources of our existence? Freud saw this as a question raised by the small child, who might fantasise that he has no parentage at all but is actually self-born. Perhaps we all sprang from our own loins, and can thus escape the indignity of being dependent for our life on others. Or perhaps, like God, there was never a moment when we were not in existence. One reason why the child might find the thought of its origins hard to bear is that whatever was born can also die. As we grow up, we must come to terms with the fact that however free and self-reliant we fancy ourselves to be, we are not in fact self-authoring. What puts us in place is a history over which we have little control, and of which we may know almost nothing. This heritage is woven into our flesh, veins, bones and organs as much as into our social conditions. We are dependent for our existence, and thus for our very freedom and autonomy, on a lineage of other individuals and events, one too tangled ever to be fully unravelled. There is a plot afoot, but it is not easy to know how we fit into it. At the root of the self is that which is not ourselves. This is a kind of conundrum we have to learn to live with.

The child might also dream that his actual family is not his real one. Perhaps he really belongs to a more glamorous set of kinsfolk altogether, and has ended up among his present relatives as a kind of changeling. Freud called this the family romance syndrome, and it is one with which Pip is clearly afflicted. Satis House represents the family he wants to be part of. This is savagely ironic, since Satis House is a rotting, poisonous, fantasy-ridden shell. Its only occupants are two solitary women, one of them probably mad and the other emotionally disabled, who have no blood-relation with each other. It is a sign of Pip's false consciousness that he should prefer this arena of sick dreams to life at the forge.

What Pip does is misread the plot of the novel. He thinks he is a character in one plot, that of Miss Havisham, but he actually belongs to another, that of Magwitch. It is never easy to say which narrative we are part of. The hero makes a disastrous mistake about the sources of his identity – about who it is that actually 'created' him. He assumes that he is the creature of Miss Havisham, but he is actually the handiwork of a convict. There is an enigma about origins, rather as Magwitch appears as a 'dreadful mystery' to Pip. Yet it is a mystery which involves more than just the individual.

Where does human civilisation itself come from? What are the sources of our common life?

The answer for this novel is unambiguous. Civilisation has its murky roots in crime, violence, labour, suffering, injustice, wretchedness and oppression. The fact that Magwitch is Pip's benefactor is symbolic of this deeper truth. It is from this coarse root that the world of civility flowers. 'I lived rough,' the convict tells Pip, 'that you should live smooth.' It is from hard labour and illegality that Pip's good fortune flows. His leisurely life in London thus has a 'taint of prison and crime' about it that he can never quite dispel. The wealth of Miss Havisham, like that of the sophisticated London world which Pip joins, also stems from wretchedness and exploitation. And the fashionable world is as unconscious of this fact, or as indifferent to it, as Pip is unaware that the underworld figure of Magwitch is the real source of his identity. Even Estella turns out to have criminal origins, as the long-lost daughter of Magwitch and a suspected murderer. It is hard to see how the civilisation portrayed in the book could survive if it were to become conscious of its true foundation.

This is an astonishingly radical view for the novel to take. In fact, it is far more radical than Dickens himself. It is a long way from his real-life political views. He was a reformist, not a revolutionary. In this sense, *Great Expectations*, like some of its author's other late novels, illustrates a point we noted earlier, that a writer's real-life opinions are not necessarily at one with the attitudes revealed in his or her work. 'Never trust the teller, trust the tale,' as D.H. Lawrence remarks. The novel's sympathies clearly lie with the criminal underworld, not with the fashionable world in which Dickens himself was so idolised. Satis House reveals the dark underside of that respectability, as Miss Havisham's greedy, hypocritical relations wait like vultures to swoop on her money when she dies.

Joe, the novel's moral touchstone, hopes that Magwitch will give the slip to the soldiers pursuing him on the marshes. When Pip arrives in London, one of the first sights he sees is Newgate prison, where the wretched inmates are whipped and hanged. Later on, when Magwitch is brought to court for sentence of execution, the novel contrasts the prisoners in the dock, 'some defiant, some stricken with terror, some sobbing and weeping, some covering their faces', with 'the sheriffs with their great chains and nosegays, other civic gewgaws and monsters, criers, ushers . . .'. There is a clear implication throughout the book that conventional society is as cruel and corrupt in its own more decorous way as the world of thieves and assassins.

The novel hints at a parallel between the child and the criminal. Both figures are half in and half out of orthodox society, stripped of privileges and sorely oppressed. Neither has the benefit of much education, and both are accustomed to being ordered about. The Victorian child may enjoy almost as little freedom as an inmate of death row. The young Pip is forever being cuffed, smacked, reproved and casually roughed up by Evangelical-minded adults for whom children are not far from the spawn of Satan. At one point, children are explicitly described as criminals fit to be hanged, which points to the secret solidarity between Pip and Magwitch. There is also a literal connection between children and crime in the novel. Jaggers, who is not exactly a bleeding-heart liberal, tells Pip indignantly how he has seen children 'being imprisoned, whipped, transported, neglected, cast out, qualified in all ways for the hangman, and growing up to be hanged'.

# Interpretation

As a feared and respected lawyer who seems to be on nodding terms with almost every ex-jailbird in London, Jaggers acts as the bridge in the story between the underworld and the overworld. His office displays the hideous death masks of hanged convicts on its walls. Since he draws part of his livelihood from death, he is also one of the book's several examples of the living dead. Magwitch, whose life as a prisoner is a living death, is another. So is Miss Havisham, frozen in the moment of her lover's betrayal, and so is Mrs Joe, who hovers somewhere between life and death after Orlick has smashed in her skull. The death of Mrs Joe suggests that Pip is not only in cahoots with a criminal. He is also indirectly responsible for murder. It was he who stole the file that Magwitch used to free himself from his leg-iron, and it was with the discarded leg-iron that Orlick attacked Mrs Joe. The shadow of matricide hangs over the hero.

* * *

The opening of *Great Expectations* sets a magnificent scene of desolation. Pip is alone on the flat, dreary, fever-breeding marshes, wandering among the tombstones of the churchyard, with a prison ship anchored offshore and a gibbet or gallows not far off. Death, crime and human misery converge in this adroitly set-up symbolism. Then Magwitch leaps out on the boy suddenly, in a moment of primordial trauma. The terrified child finds himself confronted by a monstrously alien figure, one who like many such figures in mythology is lame:

A fearful man, all in coarse grey, with a great iron on his leg. A man with no hat, and with broken shoes, and with an old rag tied round his head. A man who had been soaked in water, and smothered in mud, and lamed by stones, and cut by flints, and stung by nettles, and torn by briars; who limped, and shivered, and glared and growled; and whose teeth chattered in his head as he seized me by the chin.

There is something animal or inhuman about this dreadful apparition. Yet it is also the inhumanity of the purely human – of a man stripped of the trappings of civilisation, who makes a naked appeal to Pip's own humanity. In responding to that summons, it is as though the boy strikes a symbolic compact with all those who are outcast and dispossessed. He also establishes a secret solidarity with sin. In fact, it is not hard to read this hauntingly atmospheric scene as a narrative of the Fall, though literally speaking Pip does not so much fall as find himself turned head over heels by his desperate companion. Magwitch will indeed go on to turn Pip's world upside down as the story unfolds. It is the child's first encounter with crime and hardship, and as such the staging of a kind of original sin. All such scenes include a sense of guilt – of being caught red-handed in some terrible transgression; and Pip will soon be feeling this too, as he fears being punished for stealing from his own home. In coming to Magwitch's aid, he has fallen from innocence, even if he has done so by an act of grace. He has put himself outside the law, and however hard he tries will never be able to climb back in.

For all its compassion for the underdog, the novel refuses to idealise Magwitch. In fact, it leaves him open to some serious criticism. He is, after all, the unwitting source of much of Pip's trouble, in bestowing on him a fortune which estranges him from the forge. His generosity might well be seen as grotesquely misplaced. Pip, after all, did not ask to be made a gentleman, however much he may have welcomed the prospect at the time. Nor did Magwitch consult him on the matter. He did it for Pip's sake, but also for his own gratification. He even speaks proudly of 'owning' his protégé. There is a quiet allusion to Frankenstein and his monster. As a prisoner, Magwitch is not in command of his own existence, and he ends up by putting his beloved Pip in much the same position. In a similar way, Estella is the puppet of Miss Havisham. In the end, she turns wrathfully on her creator, and Pip does the same with Magwitch when he first returns to London. It is irresponsible of the felon to grant an almost complete stranger a share of his wealth and then simply stand back and admire his handiwork. To do so is not only to overlook the misery that wealth can bring. It is also to exercise a form of power over his spiritual adoptee. This is also glaringly true of Miss Havisham and Estella. Power lurks beneath many a relationship in this work.

There are several literary modes at work in *Great Expectations*. There is realism, but also fantasy. Miss Havisham is hardly the kind of character one might bump into in the local shopping mall, though Magwitch might make a passable security guard in such a place. Nor are the book's many contrived coincidences in the least lifelike. The novel also draws on the literary form known as the *Bildungsroman*, a tale about the education or spiritual progress of its protagonist. And there are strong elements of fable, romance, myth and fairy tale. Here, however, the novel differs from some of Dickens's earlier works. We have seen already that novels sometimes use fairy-tale devices to pull off happy endings which from a realist viewpoint seem out of reach. *Jane Eyre*, for example, reunites Jane with her stricken master by allowing her to hear his voice crying on the wind from a long way off. The early Dickens is himself a dab hand at such stratagems. *Great Expectations*, however, has seen through the fairy tale. It recognises that the bountiful fairy, Miss Havisham, is actually a wicked witch, that dreams are tainted, treasure corrupted and ambitions woven out of thin air. Abel Magwitch is an able magic witch who can transform a poor boy into a prince, but only at an appallingly steep price. The romance has turned sour. As the name 'Havisham' suggests, to have is a sham. The desire to possess is empty.

Even so, the narrative is not averse to the odd piece of manipulation. Pip does not end up back in the forge. He is allowed to live as a gentleman, though now as an industrious one. He ends up, in short, pretty much as the middle-class man he yearned to be, though now with the right values rather than the wrong ones. As far as manipulation goes, the horrific death of Miss Havisham is among other things the novel's revenge on her for her heartless designs on its hero. Pip is reconciled with Magwitch; but Magwitch dies soon after, which conveniently ensures that Pip will not be stuck with him for the rest of his days. It is one thing to clasp this coarse-mannered old codger to one's bosom, and another thing to have to put him up in the spare room for the next twenty years.

The *Bildungsroman* is above all a tale of progress, but Pip's history is one of regression. He must return to where he started in order, in the words of T.S. Eliot's *Four Quartets*, to know the place for the first time. It has been pointed out that his name is a palindrome, meaning a word which reads the same backward as well as forward; and Pip can make real progress only by journeying back to his point of origin. In order to be truly independent, you must acknowledge the unsavoury sources from which your existence stems. Only by accepting that you have a history not of your own making can you be free. By turning back to stare the past in the face, you might be able to grope tentatively forward. If you repress the past, it will only return with a vengeance to trip you up, as Magwitch bursts without warning into Pip's lodgings in London.

The novel begins with a kind of ending (the graves of Pip's parents in the churchyard) and ends with a new beginning, as a much chastened Pip and Estella step forth to start their lives afresh. Satis House, by contrast, is a place in which narrative has been suspended. Time there has come to a dead end, as Miss Havisham walks round and round her mouldering room without getting anywhere. As far as narrative goes, we may also note that though this is a tale delivered in the first person, it provides us with a morally devastating portrait of its narrator. It is a tribute to Pip's strength of character that he can see, and allow the reader to see, what an unlovable little upstart he has become. No doubt it is the same strength of character which eventually helps to pull him through.

There are some significant patterns of imagery in the story, which work to reinforce its themes. One is the image of iron, which crops up in a number of different forms: Magwitch's leg-iron, which Orlick will later to use to batter Mrs Joe; the file which Pip steals from Joe, which also reappears later in the story; the prison ship, which with its massive mooring chains seems to be 'ironed like the prisoners'; Mrs Joe's wedding ring, which scrapes the young Pip's face when she punishes him; and so on. Magwitch metaphorically forges chains for Pip, even if they are fashioned of gold and silver. Pip is legally 'bound' as an apprentice, fettered to a career as a blacksmith for which he feels nothing but contempt. Iron in the novel thus comes to symbolise violence and incarceration, but there is also a solidity and simplicity about it which contrasts with the vacuous world of Satis House and London high society. It suggests what is real about the forge and the criminal underworld, as well as what is harsh and comfortless about them.

There is also a pattern of food imagery which weaves its way through the story, and which is similarly ambiguous. Food, like iron, is associated with power and violence. Magwitch threatens to gobble the child Pip up; the pie which the boy steals for the convict becomes a source of guilt and terror for him; Mr Pumblechook recounts a bizarre tale in which Pip becomes a pig whose throat is slit; while Miss Havisham speaks of being feasted on by her predatory relatives. Yet food and drink also signify friendship and solidarity, as with Pip's generous-hearted gifts to the famished Magwitch. Dickens's heart never beats faster than when he can smell the bacon sizzling.

Nobody would guess from the account of the book I have just given that it can be ecstatically funny. Joe Gargery is among his author's finest comic creations. The novel pokes a fair amount of good-humoured fun at him, while at the same time treating him as the moral yardstick of the whole fable. The fact that Joe's forge is marooned in the countryside, however, might suggest that virtue can flourish only when isolated from corrupting social influences. The same is true of Wemmick's domestic castle. There is an abundance of humour elsewhere in the book as well. Dickens can be funny even when he is painting some deeply unpalatable realities, which suggests that one of the alternatives he is proposing to such unpleasantness is comedy itself. Goodness is in notably short supply in his later fiction; but even if there is a dearth of it in the flint-hearted world the novels portray, a good deal of moral virtue is involved in the way they portray it. The loving sympathy, imaginative flair, benevolent humour and geniality of spirit which go into the making of these fictions mean that Dickens's moral values are inseparable from the act of writing itself.

*Great Expectations* is in no doubt about which of its fictional worlds – Joe's or Miss Havisham's – is most real. *Oliver Twist*, by contrast, is in two minds about whether the criminal sub-culture of Fagin and his pack of thieving urchins is more substantial than the middle-class milieu into which Oliver is finally rescued. Is Fagin's underworld simply a nightmarish interlude, one from which you thankfully awaken in the arms of your well-heeled relatives? Or is his filthy den more solid than Brownlow's drawing room? There is something anarchically enjoyable about Fagin's way of life, which can hardly be said of the urbane lifestyle of Mr Brownlow. Fagin may be another false patriarch, but he cooks a mean sausage, which in Dickens's eyes counts heavily in his favour. He and his light-fingered apprentices may be embroiled in robbery and violence, along, no doubt, with a few less mentionable vices; but they also represent a perverse parody of a family (the only female members of it are prostitutes), and a more roisterous, fun-loving family than the Gargery set-up.

In fact, the novel's official disapproval of this pack of rascals does not quite fit with what it shows of them. Fagin may be a rogue, but like Dickens himself he is also an entertainer with an appreciative audience. When the Artful Dodger, hauled before a court, scoffs 'This ain't the shop for justice', there seems little doubt that the novel endorses his judgement. Come what may, the Dodger is going to be sent down. All the same, Brownlow and his household are genuinely caring and compassionate, as Fagin and Bill Sykes most certainly are not. Oliver has a future with them, as he does not in a thieves' kitchen. Middle-class society is not just to be dismissed as skin-deep. Its members are not all paper-thin. Civilised values of the Brownlow kind include harbouring the weak and defenceless. It is not just a question of not blowing your nose on the tablecloth.

We have seen that Pip wakes from a fever to find himself lovingly restored to Joe. Oliver, rather similarly, surfaces after a lengthy bout of illness to find himself in Brownlow's elegant home, safe for a while from Fagin's felonious clutches. Both heroes make a transition from one world to another, but in different directions. Oliver is snatched from the lower orders into civilised society, while Pip is returned from civilised society to the lower orders. That the two characters travel in opposite directions reflects different responses to the question of which sphere of life is more genuine. In a sense, though, *Great Expectations* has the best of both worlds. Pip will not stay at the forge. He will resume his life in respectable society, if on a less extravagant scale. He leaves the forge, returns, and then launches out once more. His is not exactly a tale of rags to riches and back to rags. It is more a question of from rags to a middle-of-the-range jacket and trousers.

There is, needless to say, much in this narrative that I have left unexamined. All interpretations are partial and provisional. There is no last word. It may be worth noting, however, what this brief analysis tries to do. Stepping back from the flow of the narrative, it has an eye for certain recurrent ideas and preoccupations. It notes some parallels, contrasts and connections. It tries to see character not in isolation, but as one element in a pattern which also includes theme, plot, imagery and symbolism. How language is used to create mood and emotional climate is briefly examined. The account pays some attention to the form and structure of the narrative, not just to what the story says. It considers what attitudes the novel takes up to its own characters. It glances at the various literary modes (realism, fable, fantasy, romance and so on) that are to be found in the text. Some discrepancies and ambiguities in the novel are investigated.

I also raise questions about the book's moral vision, but a reader might always want to ask how valid that vision is. Is it really true that civilisation has its roots in crime and wretchedness, or is this too jaundiced a view of it? Questions like this are perfectly legitimate. We do not have to sign on for a literary work's way of seeing. We may always complain that *Great Expectations* is too sweeping in its judgement on middle-class society, too ready to see the law as nothing but harsh and oppressive, too morbidly obsessed with death and violence, and too cosily sentimental in its handling of Joe. The fact that there is scarcely a single positive female figure in the work apart from Biddy might also claim our attention.

* * *

Both Pip and Oliver have mislaid their parents. As such, they belong to a distinguished line of orphans, semi-orphans, wards, foundlings, bastards, suspected changelings and down-in-the-mouth stepchildren who throng the pages of English literature from Tom Jones to Harry Potter. There are several reasons why orphans prove so irresistible to authors. For one thing, as deprived, often despised figures, they have to make their way in the world alone, which evokes both our sympathy and our approval. We feel for their solitude and anxiety, while admiring their efforts to haul themselves up by their bootstraps. Orphans are likely to feel vulnerable and hard done by, which can then serve as a symbolic comment on society as a whole. In Dickens's later fiction, it is as though we have all been orphaned by a social order which has abandoned its responsibilities to its citizens. Society itself is a false patriarch. All men and women have to shoulder the burden of a feckless father.

Besides, novels, not least Victorian ones, are fascinated by characters who rise from rags to riches by their own strenuous efforts. It is a dry run for the American dream. Indeed, the fact that these figures are parentless can actually smooth their progress. There is less history to hamper them. They are not caught up in a complex web of kinsfolk, but can go it alone. In D.H. Lawrence's *Sons and Lovers*, Paul Morel more or less kills off his mother. The story ends with him walking off on his own towards a more independent life. Whereas realist novels, as we have seen, tend to close with some kind of settlement, the typical modernist novel ends with someone walking away solitary and disenchanted, his problems unresolved but free of social or domestic obligations.

Orphans are anomalous figures, half in and half out of the families that take them in. They exist at an angle to their circumstances. The orphan is de trop, out of place, the joker in the domestic pack. It is this disruption that then sets the narrative in motion. So orphans prove useful devices for telling stories. If we are Victorian readers, we know that they are going to emerge at the end of the book in fine fettle, but we are curious about how the story will pull this off, and what agreeable misadventures they may meet with en route. We are thus unsettled and reassured at the same time, which is always an ambiguity to be relished. Horror movies unsettle us with their spookiness, but reassure us because we know their horror is unreal.

English literature's favourite orphan these days is indeed Harry Potter. Harry's early life with the repulsive Dursley family is not far from Pip's experience as a boy, or the young Jane Eyre's in the Reid family. In Harry's case, however, Freud's family romance syndrome actually comes true. He really does belong to a more glamorous family than the Dursleys. In fact, he discovers on first entering Hogwarts school in *Harry Potter and the Philosopher's Stone* that he is already a celebrity. He belongs to a breed of magicians who are superior not only to the Dursleys, which wouldn't be difficult, but to Muggles (non-magical humans) as such. His parents were not only accomplished wizards, but illustrious, highly respected ones. In a reversal of *Great Expectations*, the fantasy is true after all. Unlike Pip, Harry does not need to become a special person. He *is* a special person. In fact, there are unmistakable overtones of the Messiah about him, a status that not even the upwardly mobile Pip aspires to. Rather as Jaggers arrives to break the news of his great expectations to Pip, so the shaggy, gigantic Hagrid appears to reveal to Harry his true history and identity, ushering him into the privileged future prepared for him. Since Harry is a modest lad with no ambitions of his own, he is a more sympathetic figure than the uppish Pip. His good fortune is simply handed to him on a plate, without his having worked for it.

Harry has a bad substitute father in the brutish Mr Dursley, but makes up for this misfortune with a whole array of good substitute fathers, from the wise old Dumbledore to Hagrid and Sirius Black. He has a real home with the Dursleys that is no home at all, and a fantasy home (Hogwarts) where he truly belongs. The Harry Potter novels thus make a distinction between fantasy and reality, but they also bring this distinction into question. Dumbledore tells Harry that just because something is happening inside his head doesn't mean it is not real. Fantasy and everyday reality converge in the writing itself, which hovers somewhere between realism and non-realism. The books portray a realistic world in which grossly improbable events take place. Readers need to recognise their own reality in the novels so they can enjoy seeing it transformed by the power of magic. Since the majority of these readers are children, most of whom have little status or authority, seeing other children equipped with prodigious powers is no doubt particularly gratifying. So the mixture of realism and non-realism is essential, even though having the familiar and the exotic sit side by side in this way leads to incongruities on almost every page. Characters cast spells while wearing blue jeans. Broomsticks throw up dirt and pebbles when they land. The Death Eaters and Auntie Muriel exist cheek by jowl. Unreal creatures enter and exit through real doors. At one point, Harry uses his wand to clean a filthy handkerchief which he has used to scour an oven. Why not just use the wand to scour the oven?

If magic could resolve all human problems, there would be no narrative. We have seen already that for a story to get off the ground, its characters must meet with mishaps, revelations or changes of fortune. In the Potter novels, this disruption cannot arise from a clash between magic and reality, since the magic would effortlessly triumph and there would be no adventures to recount. So it must spring instead from a division within the world of magic itself, between good wizards and bad ones. Magical powers are double-edged. They can be used for evil as well as for good. Only in this way can a plot begin to unfurl. Yet this means that good and evil are not exactly the opposites they appear. They can flow from the same source. The term 'Hallows', in the title *Harry Potter and the Deathly Hallows*, comes from a word meaning to consecrate or make holy, so that it is unsettling to see it yoked so tightly to the adjective 'deathly'. It reminds us that the word 'sacred' originally meant both blessed and cursed. We have seen that the novels contrast fantasy with reality, while also showing how the two realms are intermingled. In a similar way, they insist on an absolute

conflict between the powers of light and the forces of darkness –
between the selfless Harry and the malevolent Voldemort – but at
the same time bring this antithesis into constant question.

This is apparent in a number of ways. For one thing, good father
figures like Dumbledore can come to seem malign ones. Rather
like Magwitch in *Great Expectations*, Dumbledore is at work on a
secret plot for Harry's salvation; but, as with Magwitch's plans for
Pip, we wonder at times whether his schemes are entirely well
intentioned. Dumbledore will turn out to be on the side of the
angels yet flawed, and this complicates too easy an antagonism
between good and evil. So does the ambiguous career of Severus
Snape. Besides, Voldemort is not simply Harry's enemy. He is also
his symbolic father and monstrous alter ego. The combat between
the two recalls that between Luke Skywalker and Darth Vader in
*Starwars*, right down to the V of the villain's name.

It is true that Voldemort is not Harry's actual begetter, as Darth
Vader is Luke's; but there is a vital piece of him installed inside
Harry, as there is a genetic piece of our parents inside us all. In
seeking to destroy the dark Lord, then, Harry is also doing battle
with himself. The real enemy is always the enemy within. He is
torn between his hatred for this despot and his reluctant intimacy
with him. 'I hate the fact that he can get inside me,' he protests. 'But
I'm going to use it.' Harry and Voldemort are at one level identical.
Like so many legendary rivals, they are mirror images of each other.
But Harry can seize advantage of his access to the villain's mind in
order to lay him low.

Voldemort is an image of the father as obscenely cruel and
oppressive, rather than, as with Harry's actual parents, life-giving
and affectionate. He represents the father as the forbidding Law or
superego, which for Freud is a force within the self rather than an

external authority. This dark side of the patriarchal figure is associated in Freud's thought with the threat of wounding and castration. If Harry carries a literal scar on his forehead that links him to Voldemort by a kind of psychical hotline, the rest of us may be said to bear psychological scars with similar origins. Since Voldemort wishes to claim Harry as his own, the hero becomes a battleground between the forces of light and darkness. In fact, the story avoids tragedy only by the skin of its teeth. Like many redemptive figures, Harry must die himself if he is to restore life to others. Without his own death, Voldemort cannot perish either. Yet children's stories are traditionally comic, lest toddlers are packed off to sleep quaking with trauma, so the narrative musters an array of magical devices to save Harry from this fate. Its closing words are the implicit last words of all comedy: 'All was well.'

What else might a literary critic discover in these tales? There is a political dimension to them, as a fascistic elite of magicians hostile to those of their kind with Muggle blood do battle with more enlightened wizards. This raises some important questions. How is one to be 'other' without feeling superior? How does a minority differ from an elite? Can one be set apart from the mass of men and women, as wizards and witches are from Muggles, yet maintain some solidarity with them? There is an unspoken question here concerning the relations between children and adults, of which the magicians/Muggles relationship is a kind of allegory. Children represent a kind of conundrum, being similar to adults yet different. Like the inhabitants of Hogwarts, they live in a world of their own, though one which overlaps with the adult sphere. Their differences from grown-ups must be acknowledged if they are to be valued for what they are, but not to the point where they are treated as sinisterly 'other'. This is a mistake that some Victorian

Evangelicals made, treating their offspring as wayward and unregenerate. It can also be found in some modern horror movies. There is something about the otherness of children that makes us think of aliens and evil spirits, as in *ET* and *The Exorcist*. The child as spooky is the modern equivalent of the child as sinful. Freud gave the name of the uncanny to things which were both strange and familiar. Yet if it is a mistake to imagine that all children spew multicoloured vomit at the slightest opportunity, it is equally a mistake to treat them as pocket-sized adults, as people did before what has been called the invention of childhood. (Children in English literature begin with Blake and Wordsworth.) In the same way, differences between ethnic groups need to be registered, but not to the point where one makes a fetish of otherness and obscures the vast amount they have in common.

Another noteworthy aspect of the books is the number of syllables in the names of the major characters. In England, upper-class men and women tend to have longer names than their working-class compatriots. A profusion of syllables can signal other kinds of affluence. Someone named Fiona Fortescue-Arbuthnot-Smythe is unlikely to hail from the backstreets of Liverpool, while someone called Joe Doyle might well do so. Hermione Granger, whose first name is fairly common in English upper-middle-class circles, and whose second name suggests a large country house (grange), is the most refined of the trio of protagonists, with no fewer than six syllables to her name. (Some Americans mistakenly pronounce 'Hermione' as having only three.) Harry Potter, the conventionally middle-class hero, has four neatly balanced syllables, which is neither excessive nor ungenerous, while the plebeian Ron Weasley has a niggardly three. His surname evokes the word 'weasel', meaning a treacherous or deceitful individual. Weasels are not exactly imposing beasts, and may thus conveniently lend their name to lowish-life characters like Ron.

We may also note the remarkable number of words which begin like Voldemort with V and which have negative connotations: villain, vice, vulture, vandal, venomous, vicious, venal, vain, vapid, vituperative, vacuous, voracious, vampire, virulent, vixen, voyeur, vomit, venture capitalist, vertigo, vex, vulgar, vile, viper, virago, violent, verkrampte, vindictive, vermin, vengeful, voyeur, vigilante and (for enthusiasts of traditional ways of performing Irish music) Van Morrison. A V-sign is an insulting, symbolically castrating gesture. Voldemort means 'flight of death' in French, but there may also be a suggestion of 'vole', another less-than-majestic creature. Perhaps there are also hints of 'vault' and 'mould'.

There are literary critics who would not consider the Harry Potter novels worth discussing. In their view, they are not of sufficient merit to count as literature. It is to this question of goodness and badness in literature that we can now turn.

# CHAPTER 5

# Value

What is it that makes a work of literature good, bad or indifferent? There have been many answers to this question over the centuries. Depth of insight, truth-to-life, formal unity, universal appeal, moral complexity, verbal inventiveness, imaginative vision: all of these have been proposed at one time or another as marks of literary greatness, not to speak of one or two more dubious criteria such as giving voice to the indomitable spirit of the nation, or stepping up the rate of steel production by portraying steel workers as epic heroes.

For some critics, originality counts for a good deal. The more a work can break with tradition and convention, inaugurating something genuinely new, the more likely we are to rate it highly. A number of Romantic poets and philosophers held this view. A moment's reflection, however, is enough to cast doubt on it. Not everything that is new is valuable. Chemical weapons are of recent vintage, but not many people rejoice in them for this reason. Neither is all tradition stuffy and staid. There is more to it than bank managers donning chainmail and re-enacting the battle of Hastings. There are honourable traditions, such as those of the English suffragettes or the American civil rights movement. A heritage can be revolutionary as well as backward-looking. Nor are conventions always stiff and artificial. The word 'convention' simply means 'coming together', and without such convergence there could be no social existence, let alone works of art. People make love according to convention. There is no point in spraying oneself with perfume and arranging a candle-lit dinner if one lives in a culture in which this is the customary prelude to a kidnapping.

Eighteenth-century authors like Pope, Fielding and Samuel Johnson treated originality with some suspicion. It struck them as modish, even freakish. Novelty was a kind of eccentricity. The creative imagination was dangerously close to idle fantasy. In any case, innovation was strictly speaking impossible. There could be no new moral truths. It would have been outrageously inconsiderate of God not to have revealed to us from the outset the few, simple precepts necessary for our salvation. It would have been unforgivably remiss of him to forget to tell the ancient Assyrians that adultery was a sin, and then pack them off to hell for it. In the eyes of neo-classicists like Pope and Johnson, what millions of men and women had found true over the centuries was bound to be more worthy of respect than some new-fangled notion. Nothing some wild-eyed genius might dream up at two o'clock in the morning could outweigh the common wisdom of humankind. Human nature was everywhere alike, which meant there could be no genuine advance on the way it was portrayed by Homer and Sophocles.

Science might develop, but art did not. Affinities were more noteworthy than differences, and the common more weighty than the singular. The task of art was to provide us with lively images of what we already knew. The present was for the most part a recycling of the past. It was its fidelity to the past that lent it legitimacy. The past was mostly what the present was made up of, and the future would ring a set of minor variations on what had gone before. Change was to be treated sceptically. It was more likely to represent degeneration than progress. It was, of course, inevitable, but the mutability of human affairs was a sign of our fallen condition. There was no alteration in Eden.

If this neo-classical view of the world seems light years from our own, it is partly because romanticism intervened between the two. For the Romantics, men and women are creative spirits with an inexhaustible power to transform their world. Reality is thus dynamic rather than static, and change is mostly to be celebrated rather than feared. Human beings are makers of their own history, and potentially infinite progress lies within their grasp. To embark on this brave new world, they need simply to throw off the forces which shackle them. The creative imagination is a visionary power which can remake the world in the image of our deepest desires. It inspires political revolutions as well as poems. There is a fresh emphasis on individual genius. Human beings are no longer to be seen as frail, flawed creatures, always likely to fall into error and perpetually in need of the smack of firm government. Instead, their roots run down to infinity. Freedom is of their very essence. Yearning and striving are of their nature, and their true home lies in eternity. We should cultivate a generous trust in human capabilities. The passions and affections are mostly benign. Unlike cold-hearted reason, they bind us to Nature and to each other. They should be allowed to flourish free of artificial constraint. The truly just society, as well as the finest work of art, is the one which would allow this to happen. The most cherished artworks are those which transcend tradition and convention. Instead of slavishly imitating the past, they bring to birth something rich and strange.

Each work of art is a miraculous new creation. It is an echo or repetition of God's act of creating the world. Like the Almighty, the artist conjures his or her work out of nothing. It is the imagination that inspires it, and the imagination is a matter of possibility rather than actuality. It can summon into being things that never existed before, like ancient mariners with hypnotic powers or pieces of pottery given to making philosophical statements. Even so, the artist can never quite get on terms with God, who as far as creation goes has got there first and pulled off a product hard to beat. The poet may imitate the divine act of creation, yet she does so from her restricted situation in time. In any case, this theory is plainly at odds with what writers actually get up to. No work of art springs out of nothing. Coleridge did not invent ancient mariners and Keats did not dream up Grecian urns. Like any other artist, Romantic writers forged their art out of materials which they did not manufacture themselves. In this sense, they are more like bricklayers than minor deities.

The Romantic impulse to make it new is inherited by modernism. The modernist work of art takes a stand against a world in which everything seems standardised, stereotyped and prefabricated. It gestures to a realm beyond this second-hand, ready-made civilisation. It aims to make us see the world afresh – to disrupt our routine perceptions rather than to reinforce them. In its strangeness and specificity, it tries to resist being reduced to just another commodity. Yet if a work of art were absolutely new, we would not be able to identify it at all, rather as the true aliens are not dwarfish and many-limbed but perched invisibly in our laps at this very moment. To be recognisable as art, a work must have some connection with what we categorise as art already, even if it ends up by transforming the category out of all recognition. Even a revolutionary artwork can be judged as such only by reference to what it has revolutionised.

In any case, even the most innovative literary work is made up among other things of the scraps and leavings of countless texts that have come before. The medium of literature is language, and every word we use is shop-soiled, tarnished, worn thin and feature-less by billions of previous usages. To exclaim 'My uniquely precious, unspeakably adorable darling' is always in some sense a quotation. Even if this particular sentence has never been uttered before, which is highly unlikely, it is fashioned out of materials that are drearily familiar. In this sense, conservative neo-classicists like Pope or Johnson are shrewder than they might seem. There can be no absolute novelty, as some twentieth-century avant-gardists forlornly dreamed. It is difficult to imagine a more stunningly original work than Joyce's *Finnegans Wake*. Indeed, it is hard at first glance to tell what language it is written in, let alone what it means. In fact, the *Wake* draws on a whole range of well-thumbed words. What is new is the bizarre way it combines them. In this sense, it does more flamboyantly what all literary works do all the time.

This is not to suggest that there can be no novelty at all. If there are no absolute breaks in human affairs, neither are there any abso-lute continuities. It is true that we are forever recycling our signs. But it is also true, as Noam Chomsky reminds us, that we constantly produce sentences we have never heard or spoken before. And to this extent the Romantics and modernists are in the right of it. Language is a work of astonishing creativity. It is by far the most magnificent artefact humanity has ever come up with. It even surpasses the movies of Mel Gibson in this respect. As for new truths, we discover them all the time. One name for this enquiry is science, which was in its infancy in the age of the neo-classicists.

But art, too, can innovate as well as inherit. A writer can fashion a new literary form, as Henry Fielding thought he was doing, or as Bertolt Brecht did in the theatre. Such forms have their forerunners, like most other things in human history. But they may also break genuinely new ground. Nothing quite like T.S. Eliot's *The Waste Land* had ever been seen before in the history of literature.

It is with postmodernism that the hunger for novelty begins to fade. Postmodern theory does not rate originality very highly. It has put revolution well behind it. Instead, it embraces a world in which everything is a recycled, translated, parodied or derivative version of something else. This is not to say that everything is a copy. To say so would imply that there was an original around somewhere, which is not the case. Instead, we have simulacra without an original. In the beginning was the imitation. If we were to come across what looked like an original, we could be sure that this, too, would turn out to be a copy, pastiche or piece of mimicry. This is no reason to be despondent, however, since if nothing is authentic, nothing can be fake. It would not be logically possible for everything to be bogus. A signature is the mark of one's uniquely individual presence, but it is authentic only because it looks roughly like one's other signatures. It must be a copy in order to be genuine. Everything at this late, streetwise, rather cynical point in history has been done before; but it can always be done again, and the act of doing it again is what constitutes the novelty. To copy out *Don Quixote* word for word would represent a genuine innovation. All phenomena, including all works of art, are woven out of other phenomena, so that nothing is ever quite new or ever quite the same. To steal a phrase from Joyce, postmodernism is a 'neverchanging everchanging' culture, rather as late capitalism never stays still for a moment but is never transfigured out of recognition either.

If good literature is always ground-breaking literature, we would be forced to deny the value of a great many literary works, from ancient pastoral and medieval mystery plays to sonnets and folk ballads. The same is true of the claim that the finest poems, plays and novels are those which recreate the world around us with incomparable truth and immediacy. On this theory, the only good literary texts are realist ones. Everything from the *Odyssey* and the Gothic novel to expressionist drama and science fiction would have to be written off as inferior. Lifelikeness, however, is a ridiculously inadequate yardstick for measuring literary value. Shakespeare's Cordelia, Milton's Satan and Dickens's Fagin are fascinating precisely because we are unlikely to encounter them in Walmart's. There is no particular merit in a literary work being true to life, rather as there is no necessary value in a drawing of a cork-screw that looks exactly like a corkscrew. Perhaps our delight in such resemblances is a survival of mythical or magical thought, which is much taken with affinities and correspondences. For the Romantics and modernists, the point of art is not to imitate life but to transform it.

In any case, what counts as realism is a contentious matter. We generally think of realistic characters as complex, substantial, well-rounded figures who evolve over time, like Shakespeare's Lear or George Eliot's Maggie Tulliver. Yet some of Dickens's characters are realistic precisely by being none of these things. Far from being well rounded, they are grotesque, two-dimensional caricatures of human beings. They are men and women reduced to a few offbeat features or eye-catching physical details. As one critic has pointed out, however, this is just the way we tend to perceive people on busy thoroughfares or crowded street corners. It is a typically urban way of seeing, one which belongs to the city street rather than the village green. It is as though characters loom up out of the crowd, allow us a quick, vivid impression of themselves, then disappear for ever into the throng.

In Dickens's world, this serves only to heighten their mysteriousness. Many of his characters appear secretive and inscrutable. They have a cryptic quality about them, as though their inner lives are impenetrable to others. Perhaps they have no inner life at all, being nothing but a set of surfaces. Sometimes they seem more like pieces of furniture than living beings. Or perhaps their true selves are locked away behind their appearances, beyond reach of an observer. Once again, this mode of characterisation reflects life in the city. In the anonymity of the great metropolis, individuals seem shut up in their solitary lives, with little continuous knowledge of or involvement with one another. Human contacts are fleeting and sporadic. People appear as enigmas to each other. So in portraying urban men and women as he does, Dickens is arguably more realistic than showing them in the round.

A literary work may be realist but not realistic. It may present a world which appears familiar, but in a way that is shallow and unconvincing. Slushy romances and third-rate detective stories fall into this category. Or a work may be non-realist but realistic, projecting a world unlike our own but in ways which reveal something true and significant about everyday experience. *Gulliver's Travels* is a case in point. *Hamlet* is non-realist because young men do not usually speak in verse while berating their mothers or running a sword through their prospective fathers-in-law. But the play is realistic in some more subtle sense of the word. Being true to life does not always mean being true to everyday appearances. It might mean taking them apart.

Are all major works of literature timeless and universal in their appeal? This, certainly, has been one powerful contention over the centuries. Great poems and novels are those that transcend their age and speak meaningfully to us all. They deal in the permanent, imperishable features of human existence – in joy, suffering, grief, death and sexual passion, rather than in the local and incidental. This is why we can still respond to works like Sophocles' *Antigone* and Chaucer's *Canterbury Tales*, even though they date from cultures very different from our own. On this view, there could be a great novel about sexual jealousy (Proust's *Remembrance of Things Past*, for example), but probably not about the failure of a sewage system in Ohio.

There may be something in this claim, but it raises a number of questions. *Antigone* and *Oedipus the King* have survived for thousands of years. But is the *Antigone* we admire today quite the same piece of drama that the ancient Greeks applauded? Is what we think central to it what they did too? If it is not, or if we cannot be sure, then we should hesitate before we speak of the same work enduring over centuries. Perhaps if we were really to discover what a certain ancient work of art meant to its contemporary audiences, we would cease to rate it so highly or enjoy it so much. Did the Elizabethans and Jacobeans get the same things out of Shakespeare's work as we do? No doubt there are important overlaps. But we need to recall that the average Elizabethan or Jacobean approached these plays with a set of beliefs very different from our own. And every interpretation of a literary work is coloured, however unconsciously, by our own cultural values and assumptions. Will our great-grandchildren look on Saul Bellow or Wallace Stevens as we do?

A literary classic, some critics consider, is not so much a work whose value is changeless as one that is able to generate new meanings over time. It is, so to speak, a slow-burning affair. It gathers different interpretations as it evolves. Like an ageing rock star, it can adapt itself to new audiences. Even so, we should not assume that such classics are up and running all the time. Like business enterprises, they can close down and start up again. Works may pass in and out of favour according to changing historical circumstances. Some eighteenth-century critics were far less enraptured by Shakespeare or Donne than we are today. Quite a few of them would not have counted drama as literature at all, not even bad literature. They would probably have had similar reservations about the vulgar, upstart, mongrelised form known as the novel. Samuel Johnson wrote of Milton's *Lycidas*, the opening of which we glanced at in the first chapter, that 'the diction is harsh, the rhymes uncertain, and the numbers unpleasing ... In this poem there is no nature, for there is no truth; there is no art, for there is nothing new. Its form is that of a pastoral, easy, vulgar, and therefore disgusting.' Yet Johnson is generally agreed to be a supremely capable critic.

Changes of historical circumstance may result in works falling into disfavour. There could be no valuable Jewish writing for the Nazis. A general shift of sensibility means that we no longer prize didactic writing very highly, though the sermon was once a major genre. There is, in fact, no reason to suppose, as modern readers often do, that literature which tries to teach us something is likely to be tedious. We moderns tend to be averse to 'doctrinal' literature, but *The Divine Comedy* is exactly that. The doctrinal need not be dogmatic. Our own heartfelt convictions may appear like arid doctrines to someone else. Novels and poems may deal with subjects that were of pressing concern when they were written but no longer strike us as of earth-shattering importance. Tennyson's *In*

*Memoriam* frets about evolutionary theory, as most of us today do not. There are some problems that are simply no longer problems, even if they have not been adequately resolved. On the other hand, works which have fallen into near-oblivion may be jolted into fresh life by historical developments. In the crisis of Western civilisation that culminated in the First World War, metaphysical poets and Jacobean dramatists who had also lived through a time of social turmoil were suddenly back in favour. With the rise of modern feminism, Gothic novels with persecuted heroines ceased to be regarded as minor curios and acquired a new centrality.

The fact that a work of literature deals in permanent features of the human condition, such as death, suffering or sexuality, does not guarantee it major status. It may deal with these things in a supremely trivial way. In any case, these universal aspects of humanity tend to assume different forms in different cultures. Death for an agnostic age like our own is not quite what it was for St Augustine or Julian of Norwich. Grief and mourning are common to all peoples. Yet a literary work might express them in such a culturally specific form that it fails to engage our interest at all deeply. Anyway, why couldn't there be a great play or novel about the failure of a sewage system in Ohio, which is scarcely a permanent feature of the human condition? Why might it not be of potentially universal interest? After all, the feelings inspired by such a failure – anger, alarm, guilt, remorse, anxiety about human contamination, fear of waste products and so on – are shared by many different civilisations.

In fact, one problem with the case that all great works of litera-ture deal in the universal rather than the local is that very few human emotions are confined to specific cultures. There are, to be sure, some instances of what one might call local emotions. Modern

Western males are not as touchy about their honour as medieval knights seem to have been. Neither are they much motivated by the laws of chivalry. A modern Western woman would not feel polluted by marrying her deceased husband's first cousin, as might well be the case in a tribal society. For the most part, however, passions and sentiments cross cultural boundaries. One reason for this is that they are bound up with the human body, and the body is what human beings have most fundamentally in common.

What we have in common, however, is not our only concern. We are fascinated by what differs from us as well. It is this that the champions of universality sometimes fail to recognise. We do not generally read travel literature to reassure ourselves that the Tongans or Melanesian islanders feel just the same way about insider trading as we do. Not many fans of the Icelandic sagas claim that they have a bearing on the agricultural policies of the European Union. If we are inspired only by literature that reflects our own interests, all reading becomes a form of narcissism. The point of turning to Rabelais or Aristophanes is as much to get outside our own heads as to delve more deeply into them. People who see themselves everywhere are a bore.

How far a literary work speaks to more than its own historical situation may depend on that situation. If, for example, it springs from a momentous era in human history, one in which men and women are living through some world-shaking transition, it might be animated by this fact to the point where it also appeals to readers in very different times and places. The Renaissance and the Romantic period are obvious examples. Literary works which transcend their historical moment may do so because of the nature of that moment, as well as of the specific way they belong to it. The writings of Shakespeare, Milton, Blake and Yeats resonate so deeply of their own times and places that they can echo down the centuries and across the globe.

No work of literature is literally timeless. They are all products of specific historical conditions. To call some books timeless is just a way of saying that they tend to hang around a lot longer than ID cards or shopping lists. Even then, however, they may not hang around forever. Only on Judgement Day will we know if Virgil or Goethe managed to make it through to the end of time, or whether J.K. Rowling beat Cervantes by a short head. There is also the question of spread in space. If great works of literature are universal, then presumably Stendhal or Baudelaire must in principle speak as relevantly to the Dinka or Dakota as they do to Westerners, or at least to some Westerners. It is true that a Dinka might come to appreciate Jane Austen just as well as a Mancunian. To do so, however, he or she would need to learn the English language, gain some knowledge of the Western novel form, grasp something of the historical background against which Austen's fiction makes sense, and so on. To understand a language is to understand a form of life.

The same would be true of an English reader intent on exploring the riches of Inuit poetry. In both cases, one needs to reach beyond one's own cultural environs to enjoy the art of another civilisation. There is nothing impossible about that. People do it all the time. But there is more to understanding the art of another culture than there is to understanding a theorem produced by its mathematicians. You can grasp a language only by grasping more than a language. Nor is it true that Austen is meaningful to other societies simply because everyone, English, Dinka and Inuit alike, shares the same humanity. Even if they do, it would not be sufficient grounds for them to enjoy *Pride and Prejudice*.

What does it mean in any case to rank a literary work as great? Almost everyone would assign this distinction to Dante's *Divine Comedy*, but this may be more of a nominal judgement than a real one. It might be like seeing that someone is sexually attractive but not feeling sexually attracted to them. For the great majority of modern men and women, Dante's world view is too alien for his poetry to yield them much pleasure or insight. They might still acknowledge that he is a magnificent poet; but they are unlikely to *feel* this to be true, in the way they might feel it to be true of Hopkins or Hart Crane. People may continue to tip their hats to such classics long after they have ceased to mean much to them. Yet if absolutely nobody was enthused by *The Divine Comedy* any more, it would be hard to know how it could still be said to be a great poem.

You can also reap pleasure from a literary work you regard as fairly worthless. There are plenty of action-packed books in airport bookstores which people devour without imagining they are in the presence of great art. Perhaps there are professors of literature who lap up the adventures of Rupert Bear by torchlight under the bedclothes at night. Enjoying a piece of art is not the same as admiring it. You can enjoy books you do not admire and admire books you do not enjoy. Dr Johnson had a high opinion of *Paradise Lost*, but one has the distinct feeling that he would have been reluctant to plough through it again.

Enjoyment is more subjective than evaluation. Whether you prefer peaches to pears is a question of taste, which is not quite true of whether you think Dostoevsky a more accomplished novelist than John Grisham. Dostoevsky is better than Grisham in the sense that Tiger Woods is a better golfer than Lady Gaga. Anyone who understands fiction or golf well enough would be almost bound to sign up to such judgements. There comes a point at which not recognising that, say, a certain brand of malt whisky is of world-class quality means not understanding malt whisky. A true knowledge of malts would include the ability to make such discriminations.

Does this then mean that literary judgements are objective? Not in the sense that 'Mount Olympus is taller than Woody Allen' is objective. If literary judgements were objective in that sense there would be no arguing over them, and you can wrangle far into the night over whether Elizabeth Bishop is a finer poet than John Berryman. Yet reality does not divide neatly down the middle between objective and subjective. Meaning is not subjective, in the sense that I cannot just decide that the warning 'Smoking Kills' on a cigarette packet really means 'Nicotine Helps Kids Grow, So Share These Ciggies with your Toddler!' Yet 'Smoking Kills' means what it means only by force of social convention. There may be a language somewhere in the cosmos in which it means a song for several voices, typically unaccompanied and arranged in elaborate counterpoint.

The point is that there are criteria for determining what counts as excellence in golf or fiction, as there are not for determining whether peaches taste better than pineapples. And these criteria are public, not just a question of what one happens privately to prefer. You have to learn how to handle them by sharing in certain social practices. In the case of literature, these social practices are known as literary criticism. This still leaves a lot of room for dissent and disagreement. Criteria are guides for how to go about making value judgements. They do not make them for you, any more than following the rules of chess will win the game for you. Chess is played not just according to rules, but by the creative application of such rules; and the rules themselves will not tell you how to apply them creatively. That is a matter of know-how, intelligence and experience. Knowing what counts as excellence in fiction is likely to decide the issue between Chekhov and Jackie Collins, but not between Chekhov and Turgenev.

Different cultures may have different criteria for deciding what counts as good or bad art. As a foreign onlooker, you might be present at some ceremony in a Himalayan village and say whether you found it boring or exhilarating, high-spirited or stiffly ritualised. What you could not say was whether it was well executed. To judge that would involve having access to the standards of excellence appropriate to that particular activity. The same goes for works of literature. Standards of excellence may also differ from one kind of literary art to another. What makes for a fine piece of pastoral is not what makes for a powerful piece of science fiction.

Works which are deep and complex would seem obvious candidates for literary merit. Yet complexity is not a value in itself. The fact that something is complex does not automatically earn it a place among the immortals. The muscles of the human leg are complex, but those with calf injuries might prefer them not to be. The plot of *Lord of the Rings* is complex, but this is not enough to endear Tolkien's work to those who dislike donnish escapism or medievalist whimsy. The point of some lyrics and ballads is not their complexity but their poignant simplicity. Lear's cry of 'Never, never, never, never, never' is not exactly complex, and is all the finer for it.

Nor is it true that all good literature is profound. There can be a superb art of the surface, such as Ben Jonson's comedies, Oscar Wilde's high-society dramas or Evelyn Waugh's satires. (We should beware, however, of the prejudice that comedy is always less deep an affair than tragedy. There are some searching comedies and some trite tragedies. Joyce's *Ulysses* is a profound piece of comedy, which is not the same as saying that it is profoundly funny, even though it is.) Surfaces are not always superficial. There are literary forms in which complexity would be out of place. *Paradise Lost* reveals little psychological depth or intricacy, and neither do Robert Burns's lyrics. Blake's 'Tyger' poem is deep and complex, but not psychologically so.

Plenty of critics, as we have seen, insist that good art is coherent art. The most accomplished works of literature are the most harmoniously unified. In an impressive economy of technique, every detail pulls its weight in the overall design. One problem with this claim is that 'Little Bo Peep' is coherent but banal. Besides, many an effective postmodern or avant-garde work is centreless and eclectic, made up of parts that do not slot neatly together. They are not necessarily any the worse for that. There is no virtue in harmony or cohesion as such, as I have suggested already. Some of the great artworks of the Futurists, Dadaists and Surrealists are deliberately dissonant. Fragmentation can be more fascinating than unity.

Perhaps what makes a work of literature exceptional is its action and narrative. Certainly Aristotle thought that a solid, well-wrought action was central to at least one species of literary writing (tragedy). Yet nothing much happens in one of the greatest plays of the twentieth century (*Waiting for Godot*), one of the finest novels (*Ulysses*) and one of the most masterly poems (*The Waste Land*). If a sturdy plot and a strong narrative are vital to literary status, Virginia Woolf sinks to a dismally low place in the league tables. We no longer rate a substantial plot as highly as Aristotle did. In fact, we no longer insist on a plot or narrative at all. Unless we are small children, we are less enamoured of stories than our ancestors. We also recognise that compelling art can be spun out of meagre materials.

What, then, of linguistic quality? Do all great literary works use language in resourceful and inventive ways? It is surely a virtue of literature that it restores human speech to its true abundance, and in doing so recovers something of our suppressed humanity. A good deal of literary language is copious and exuberant. As such, it can act as a critique of our everyday utterances. Its eloquence can issue a rebuke to a civilisation for which language has become for the most part crudely instrumental. Soundbites, text-speak, managerial jargon, tabloid prose, political cant and bureaucratese can be shown up for the bloodless forms of discourse they are. Hamlet's last words are 'Absent thee from felicity awhile, / And in this harsh world draw thy breath in pain, / To tell my story . . . the rest is silence.' Steve Jobs's last words were 'Oh wow, oh wow, oh wow.' Some might feel that there has been a certain falling-off here. Literature is about the felt experience of language, not just the practical use of it. It can draw our attention to the opulence of a medium that we usually take for granted. Poetry is concerned not just with the meaning of experience, but with the experience of meaning.

Even so, not everything we call literary has a sumptuous way with words. There are literary works that do not use language in particularly eye-catching ways. A good deal of realist and naturalistic fiction employs a plain, sober speech. One would not describe the poetry of Philip Larkin or William Carlos Williams as lushly metaphorical. George Orwell's prose is not exactly luxuriant. There is not much burnished rhetoric in Ernest Hemingway. The eighteenth century valued a lucid, exact, serviceable prose. Works of literature should certainly be well written, but then so should all writing, including memos and menus. You do not have to sound like *The Rainbow* or *Romeo and Juliet* to qualify as a reputable piece of literature.

So what makes such works good or bad? We have seen that some common assumptions on this score do not bear much scrutiny. Perhaps, then, we can cast more light on the question by analysing some literary extracts with an eye to how well they do.

* * *

We may begin with a sentence from John Updike's novel *Rabbit at Rest*: 'A shimmery model, skinny as a rail, dimpled and square-jawed like a taller Audrey Hepburn from the *Breakfast at Tiffany* days, steps out of the car, smiling slyly and wearing a racing driver's egg-helmet with her gown made up it seems of ropes of shimmering light.' Apart from one rather careless near-repetition ('shimmery', 'shimmering'), this is a highly accomplished piece of writing. Too accomplished, one might feel. It is too clever and calculated by half. Every word seems to have been meticulously chosen, polished, slotted neatly together with the other words and then smoothed over to give a glossy finish. There is not a hair out of place. The sentence is too *voulu*, too carefully arranged and displayed. It is trying too hard. There is nothing spontaneous about it. It has the air of being over-crafted, as every word is put fastidiously to work, with no loose ends or irregularities. As a result, the piece is artful but lifeless. The adjective 'slick' springs to mind. The passage is meant to be a bit of detailed description, but there is so much going on at the level of language, so many busy adjectives and piled-up clauses, that it is hard for us to concentrate on what is being portrayed. The language draws the reader's admiring attention to its own deftness. Perhaps we are particularly invited to admire the way it propels itself through so many sub-clauses, all draped around the main verb 'steps', without for a moment losing its balance.

There is a lot of such stuff in Updike's fiction. Take this portrait of a female character from the same novel:

Pru has broadened without growing heavy in that suety Pennsylvania way. As if invisible pry bars have slightly spread her bones and new calcium been wedged in and the flesh gently stretched to fit, she now presents more front. Her face, once narrow like Judy's, at moments looks like a flattened mask. Always tall, she has in the years of becoming a hardened wife and matron allowed her long straight hair to be cut and teased out into bushy wings a little like the hairdo of the Sphinx.

'Like the hairdo of the Sphinx' is a pleasing imaginative touch. Once again, however, the passage draws discreet attention to its own cleverness in the act of sketching Pru. This is 'fine writing' with a vengeance. The phrase 'in that suety Pennsylvania way' is rather too knowing, and the image of the pry bars is striking but too contrived. 'Contrived', in fact, is a suitable word for this style of writing as a whole, as Pru herself threatens to disappear beneath the density of detail with which she is overlaid. The passage has the effect of describing an object rather than a person. Its style freezes a living woman into a still life.

Contrast Updike's prose with this extract from Evelyn Waugh's short story 'Tactical Exercise':

They arrived on a gusty April afternoon after a train journey of normal discomfort. A taxi drove them eight miles from the station, through deep Cornish lanes, past granite cottages and disused, archaic tin-workings. They reached the village which gave the house its postal address, passed through it and out along a track which suddenly emerged from its high banks into open grazing land on the cliff's edge, high, swift clouds and sea-birds wheeling overhead, the turf at their feet alive with fluttering wild flowers, salt in the air, below them the roar of the Atlantic breaking on the rocks, a middle-distance of indigo and white tumbled waters and beyond it the serene arc of the horizon. Here was the house.

It is not a passage that leaps from the page. It has none of the self-conscious sculpturedness of the Updike piece, and is surely all the better for it. Waugh's prose is crisp, pure and economical. It is reticent and unshowy, as though unaware of the skill with which, for example, it manages to steer a single sentence from 'They reached the village' to 'the serene arc of the horizon' through so many sub-clauses with no sense of strain or artifice. This sense of expansiveness, of both syntax and landscape, is counterpointed by the terse 'Here was the house', which signals a halt both in the story and in the way it is being delivered. 'A train journey of normal discomfort' is a pleasantly sardonic touch. 'Archaic' might be an adjective too far, but the rhythmic balance of the lines is deeply admirable. There is an air of quiet efficiency about the whole extract. The landscape is portrayed in a set of quick, deft strokes which brings it alive without cluttering the text with too much detail.

Waugh's prose has an honesty and hard-edged realism about it which show up well in contrast to Updike. They also compare well in this respect with the following extract from William Faulkner's novel *Absalom, Absalom!*:

In the overcoat buttoned awry over the bathrobe he looked huge and shapeless like a dishevelled bear as he stared at Quentin (the Southerner, whose blood ran quick to cool, more supple to compensate for violent changes in temperature perhaps, perhaps merely nearer the surface) who sat hunched in his chair, his hands thrust into his pockets as if he were trying to hug himself warm between his arms, looking somehow fragile and even wan in the lamplight, the rosy glow which now had nothing of warmth, coziness, in it, while both their breathing vaporized faintly in the cold room where there was now not two of them but four, the two who breathed not individuals now yet something both more and less than twins, the heart and blood of youth. Shreve was nineteen, a few months younger than Quentin. He looked exactly nineteen; he was one of those people whose correct age you never know because they look exactly that and so you tell yourself that he or she cannot possibly be that because he or she looks too exactly that not to take advantage of the appearance: so you never believe implicitly that he or she is either that age which they claim or that which in sheer desperation they agree to or which someone else reports them to be.

This kind of prose, much favoured by some American creative writing courses, has an air of spontaneity about it which is almost entirely fabricated. Despite its casual way with order and convention, it is as artificial as a Petrarchan sonnet. There is something fussy and affected about the way it strives to sound natural. Its air of artlessness is too self-regarding. What is really a kind of clumsiness ('where there was now not two of them') is passed off as having the rough edge of real experience. An attempt at impressive intricacy in the final lines comes through as pedantic cleverness.

The lines know nothing of tact and reticence. They sacrifice elegance, rhythm and economy to a kind of writing which (as someone once remarked of history) is just one damn thing after another. The passage is too garrulous by half. This is the kind of author whom it would be ferociously hard to shut up. And how on earth can one look exactly nineteen?

It is possible for a style to be 'literary' and effective at the same time, as this passage from Vladimir Nabokov's *Lolita*, in which the hero's car is being tailed by a private detective, may illustrate:

> The driver behind me, with his stuffed shoulders and Trappish moustache, looked like a display dummy, and his convertible seemed to move only because an invisible rope of silent silk connected it with our own shabby vehicle. We were many times weaker than his splendid, lacquered machine, so that I did not even attempt to outspeed him. *O lente currite noctis equi!* O softly run, nightmares! We climbed long grades and rolled downhill again, and heeded speed limits, and spared slow children and reproduced in sweeping terms the black wiggles of curves on their yellow shields, and no matter how and where we drove, the enchanted interspace slid on intact, mathematical, mirage-like, the viatic counter-part of a magic carpet.

At first glance, this may strike the reader as not all that remote from the Updike passage. It has a similar literary self-consciousness, as well as the same artful, fastidious attention to detail. Like Updike, too, Nabokov writes with a vigilant ear for the sound pattern of his prose. The difference lies partly in Nabokov's air of playfulness, as if the passage is amusedly aware of its own over-civilised quality. There is a faint sense that the narrator,

Humbert Humbert, is sending himself up. The ridiculous name Humbert Humbert is itself a joke at his own expense. The playfulness is there in the idea that the car 'reproduced in sweeping terms the black wiggles of curves on their yellow shields', meaning that it followed the curves in the road represented by the wiggles on the yellow roadsigns, but on a larger scale than the wiggles themselves. There is also some subtle wordplay in Humbert's creative mistranslation of Ovid's '*noctis equi* (horses of the night)' as 'nightmares'.

There is a comic discrepancy in the passage between the everyday act of driving on a US freeway and the kid-gloved, high-toned language ('invisible rope of silent silk', 'splendid, lacquered machine') in which it is described. It is a precious style of writing, meaning one which is affectedly elegant or over-refined; but the passage gets away with it partly because it is mildly amusing, partly because it is ironically self-aware, and partly because it comes through as the speaker's rather poignant way of compensating for the somewhat sordid predicament in which he finds himself, driving along with a teenage girl who is the object of his middle-aged lust and whom he has effectively hijacked. The freeway becomes an 'enchanted interspace . . . the viatic counter-part of a magic carpet' ('viatic' comes from the Latin word for 'road'). One notes how the *c* and *p* of 'counter-part' are echoed in the word 'carpet'. This highly wrought, slightly camp literary language really belongs to Humbert Humbert, the cultivated, old-fashioned narrator of the book. It marks his ironic distance from the landscape of everyday American culture through which he is moving, dragged there in his sexual pursuit of Lolita. He is fully aware of the pathetic, humiliated, out-of-place figure he cuts, as a high-minded European scholar adrift in a desert of hamburger joints and cheap motels. And this tension between him and his surroundings is reflected in the prose style.

Despite his high-mindedness, Humbert ends up pumping bullets into Quilty, a sexual rival of his, and killing him. The scene is stunning enough to be worth quoting at length:

My next bullet caught him somewhere in the side, and he rose from his chair higher and higher, like old, grey, mad Nijinski, like Old Faithful, like some old nightmare of mine, to a phenomenal altitude, or so it seemed – as he rent the air – still shaking with the rich black music – head thrown back in a howl, hand pressed to his brow, and with his other hand clutching his armpit as if stung by a hornet, down he came on his heels and, again a normal robed man, scurried out into the hall . . .

Suddenly dignified, and somewhat morose, he started to walk up the broad stairs, and, shifting my position, but not actually following him up the stairs, I fired three or four times in quick succession, wounding him at every blaze; and every time I did it to him, that horrible thing to him, his face would twitch in an absurd clownish manner, as if he were exaggerating the pain; he slowed down, rolled his eyes half closing them and made a feminine 'ah!' and he shivered every time a bullet hit him as if I were tickling him, and every time I got him with those slow, clumsy, blind bullets of mine, he would say under his breath, with a phoney British accent – all the while dreadfully twitching, shivering, smirking, but withal talking in a curiously detached and even amiable manner: 'Ah, that hurts, sir, enough! Ah, that hurts atrociously, my dear fellow. I pray you, desist. Ah, very painful, very painful indeed . . .'

It is not quite the gunfight at the OK Corral. On the contrary, it is one of the most disturbingly quirky descriptions of a murder in the history of English literature. What makes it so grotesque is the tension between the shooting itself and the absurdly prissy way in which the victim reacts to it. It is as though Quilty is performing for an audience, rather as the novel itself is doing. He is able to assume a British accent even while his blood leaks on to the stairs. Just as Nabokov's own style in the previous passage detaches itself with ironic amusement from what it is describing, so Quilty persists with his smirkings and courteously archaic phrases ('I pray you, desist') even as the narrator's bullets rip him apart. In both cases, there is a discrepancy between the reality and how it is presented.

The narrator's style in this passage is as dissociated from the bloody event as the victim himself. There is a shocking contrast between the fury and despair which drive him to murder and the primly abstract language ('to a phenomenal altitude') in which he portrays the incident. Even as he is pumping bullet after bullet into his antagonist, he cannot resist a cultural allusion to a renowned Russian dancer ('like old, grey, mad Nijinski'). The way Quilty is thrown through the air by the impact of the shot is wittily converted into a graceful leap in ballet, rather as the extract itself converts a squalid slaying into art of the highest order. One notes the beautifully, comically understated touch 'somewhat morose', as though Quilty's reaction to being filled with lead is to feel a bit down in the mouth. 'as if I were tickling him' is another splendid piece of understatement. Perhaps the most remarkable aspect of the whole passage is that it was written by an author whose first language was not English.

Nabokov's writing is full-bloodedly 'literary' without being cluttered or claustrophobic. The American author Carol Shields can write an equally 'literary' prose, but in more subdued vein. Take this passage from her novel *The Republic of Love*, whose heroine Fay McLeod is a feminist scholar researching into mermaids:

A few years ago a man called Morris Kroger gave Fay a small Inuit carving, a mermaid figure, fattish and cheerful, lying on her side propped up by her own thick muscled elbow. It is made of highly polished gray soapstone, and its rather stunted tail curls upward in an insolent flick . . .

In the matter of mermaid tails there is enormous variation. Tails may start well above the waist, flow out of the hips, or extend in a double set from the legs themselves. They're silvery with scales or dimpled with what looks like a watery form of cellulite. A mermaid's tail can be perfunctory or hugely long and coiled, suggesting a dragon's tail, or a serpent's, or a ferociously writhing penis. These tails are packed, muscular, impenetrable, and give powerful thrust to the whole of the body. Mermaid bodies are hard, rubbery, and indestructible, whereas human bodies are as easily shattered as meringues.

This is superlative literary art, but it does not draw undue attention to itself. It manages to be poetic and colloquial at the same time. This is partly because the imagery is strikingly well wrought, while the tone is fairly casual and downbeat. 'They're silvery with scales or dimpled with what looks like a watery form of cellulite' is full of fine imaginative touches, not least the word 'dimpled' and the inventive cellulite image. In a mischievous stroke, the idea that mermaids might have cellulite tugs these mysterious creatures down to our own unglamorous level. 'Fattish and cheerful' is another such piece of brisk irreverence. Yet one could imagine the sentence about cellulite being spoken in everyday conversation (note the colloquial 'They're'), though perhaps more in a senior common room than in a bowling alley.

'Its rather stunted tail curls upward in an insolent flick' is a beautifully economical phrase, one in which every word pulls its full weight. 'Insolent' in particular is delightfully unexpected. Perhaps the mermaid is giving the tail, as humans beings are said to give the finger. Or perhaps the tail is insolent because it casually disrespects our expectation that it will be fuller and longer. Comparing some mermaids' tails to a ferociously writhing penis sounds like a piece of insolence on the novel's own part, as it describes these feminine bodies by reference to the male member. 'Packed', 'muscular', 'hard' and 'powerful thrust' do this too, but 'impenetrable' comes as a surprise. We are presented with the paradox of an impenetrable organ of penetration. Mermaids are females with penis-like tails, but because their tails are like penetrating organs, they themselves are sexually impenetrable. The novel goes on to speak of them as asexual, 'there being no feminine passage designed for ingress and egress'. (The clinical language of this phrase reflects the fact that Fay writes scholarly papers on mermaids. One might come across such words written, but hardly spoken.) Because mermaids have 'hard, rubbery, and indestructible' bodies, they offer an image of strong women. One might claim that the difference between mermaids and some radical feminists is that the former cannot be penetrated while the latter do not care to be. Yet women are human, and human bodies are 'as easily shattered as meringues', so women are fragile as well as powerful. The meringue image is another splendidly imaginative stroke. Bodies, like meringues, are sweet but brittle. They can crumble to pieces in your hands. Human beings are precious, but break as easily as things of little value. Fay herself is both vital and vulnerable.

\* \* \*

Let us turn for a moment from prose to poetry. Here is a verse from Algernon Charles Swinburne's *Atalanta in Calydon*:

> *The full streams feed on flower of rushes,*
> > *Ripe grasses trammel a travelling foot,*
> *The faint fresh flame of the young year flushes*
> > *From leaf to flower and flower to fruit;*
> *And fruit and leaf are as gold and fire,*
> *And the oat is heard above the lyre,*
> *And the hoofed heel of a satyr crushes*
> > *The chestnut-husk at the chestnut-root.*

There is a certain breathless beauty about this, but it comes from not seeing anything very clearly. The lines are the verbal equivalent of a visual blur. Everything is too sweet, too lyrical and too cloying. Nothing can be seen with exactness because everything is remorselessly sacrificed to sound effect. The verse is clogged with repetition and alliteration, which rises to a peak of absurdity in 'The faint fresh flame of the young year flushes'. The description exists mostly for the sake of creating a sonorous musical texture. Every phrase is self-consciously 'poetic'. 'Ripe grasses trammel a travelling foot' is just a fancy way of saying that your foot gets caught in the grass as you walk. The tone is too rhapsodic, and the language too monotone. There is a shimmering sheen to the lines, but beneath it they are brittle. The slightest gust of reality, one feels, would bring this brittle literary creation toppling to the earth.

Despite the fervour of the feeling, Swinburne's language is notably abstract. He uses general nouns like 'leaf', 'flower', 'fruit' and 'fire'. Nothing is seen in close-up. Contrast this with a verse from Amy Lowell's poem 'The Weather-Cock Points South':

> *White flower,*
> *Flower of wax, of jade, of unstreaked agate;*
> *Flower with surfaces of ice,*
> *With shadows faintly crimson.*
> *Where in all the garden is there such a flower?*
> *The stars crowd through the lilac leaves*
> *To look at you.*
> *The low moon brightens you with silver.*

The poet's eye here is steadily on the object. The lines resonate with wonder and admiration, but their emotions are kept in check by the demands of precise description. The poem allows itself a minor flight of fancy with 'The stars crowd through the lilac leaves / To look at you', but otherwise it subordinates the imaginative to the real. 'The low moon brightens you with silver' makes it sound as though the moon is paying homage to the flower, but if this is fanciful it is also a statement of fact. Swinburne's poem is full of hypnotically repetitive rhythms, stringing together phrases with too many syllables in them, whereas the rhythms of Lowell's piece are taut and restrained. There is a control and economy about her language. Though she is moved by the beauty of the flower, she refuses to lose her cool. Swinburne's lines tumble hectically along, while Lowell weighs and balances every phrase.

# Value

We may end with a poet whose status is not in doubt. In fact, there is well-nigh universal agreement on the value of his work. So much so, indeed, that it is doubtful that his memory will ever fade. Much anthologised, he has a seat among the immortals as secure as Rimbaud or Pushkin, and his reputation has never suffered the ups and downs of some fellow writers. I am referring to the nineteenth-century Scottish poet William McGonagall, by common consent one of the most atrocious writers ever to set pen to paper. Here is an extract from his 'Railway Bridge of the Silvery Tay':

*Beautiful new railway bridge of the silvery Tay,*
*With your strong brick piers and buttresses in so grand array;*
*And your thirteen central girders, which seem to my eye,*
*Strong enough all windy storms to defy.*

*And as I gaze at thee my heart feels gay,*
*Because thou art the greatest railway bridge of the present day;*
*And can be seen from miles away,*
*From north, south, east, or west of the Tay . . .*

*Beautiful new railway bridge of the silvery Tay,*
*With your beautiful side screens along your railway;*
*Which would be a great protection on a windy day,*
*So as the railway carriages won't be blown away . . .*

The world is stuffed with mediocre poets, but it takes a certain sublime ineptitude to rival McGonagall's astonishing achievement. To be so unforgettably awful is a privilege bestowed on only a few. With magnificent consistency, he never deviates from the most abysmal standards. Indeed, he can justly boast of never having penned an indifferent or unremarkable line. It is idle to ask whether someone could write like this yet be aware of how dreadful he was. Like the less competent performers on TV talent shows, the fact that he does not know how bad he is is part of his badness.

Yet a nagging question remains. Imagine some community, perhaps in the far-flung future, in which the English language was still in use, but its resonances and conventions, maybe because of some momentous historical transformation, were very different from the English of today. Perhaps phrases like 'And can be seen from miles away' would not sound particularly lame; rhymes like 'Tay', 'railway', 'day' and 'away' would not appear absurdly repetitive; and the flat literalism and rhythmical clumsiness of 'With your strong brick piers and buttresses in so grand array' might come through as rather charming. If Samuel Johnson could complain about some of Shakespeare's most inventive imagery, is it entirely out of the question that one day McGonagall might be hailed as a major poet?

# Index

# Index

# Index

# Index

# Index

# Index

# Index

# Index

Pope, Alexander 55, 58, 176, 179
postmodernism 105
    and originality 180
prejudice *see* bias and narrative
Price, Fanny (character) *see* Austen,
    *Mansfield Park*
primitivism and progress in modernist
    novel 109–10
private and public spheres 64, 153–4
problem-solving and realist novel 104–5
progress and modernist disillusion
    109–10
propriety as influence 34–5
Proust, Marcel 125, 183
psychoanalytical thought 142
    *see also* Freud, Sigmund
psychology and character
    lack of interest in 64–5
    and modernist works 66, 67–8
public and private spheres 64, 153–4

quality of literature *see* value
questions
    and interpretation 128–34
    in William Shakespeare's *Macbeth*
        15–16
    and opening of Flann O'Brien's *Third
        Policeman* 39–40

Rankin, Ian 115
readers
    author's address to 23–4, 88
    author's attitude and interpretation
        148–9
    and creation of meaning 124–5, 146
    reception of literary work over time
        59, 146, 184–6, 206
realist literature
    and acknowledgement of reader 24
    and character 63–4, 65, 75
    illusion of reality 122, 127
    impossibility of narrating reality
        111–14
    and language 192–3
    and literary value 181–2, 194–5
    narrative and reward of virtue 101–2,
        103

problem-solving approach 104–5
    transparent language and meaning
        125–6, 131
reality and fiction
    and address to reader 24–5
    audience of spell of the play 6–7
    and character 45–8, 63–4
    elusiveness of truth 110–11,
        127–8
    everyday life and narrative 99–100
    fantasy in J.K. Rowling's *Harry Potter*
        novels 169–70
    fiction of happy endings 102, 103,
        104, 161
    impossibility of narrating reality
        111–14
    and language 126, 127–8
    modernist view of world 105–7
    narrator's authority 80–1, 83
    and opportunity 78–9
    real-life figures in fiction 41
    truth and fiction writing 121–3
    and ways of reading 2–3
reception of literary work over time 59,
    146, 184–6, 206
Rendell, Ruth 115
rhythm 10, 20–1, 204
    *see also* metre
Richardson, Samuel
    *Clarissa* 53, 94, 123, 142
        character of Clarissa 53, 94
    *Pamela* 52, 53
rogues and villains
    in J.K. Rowling's *Harry Potter* novels
        171–2
    as interesting characters 50–1, 165
    and just deserts 102
Romanticism 57–8, 78, 135
    and originality 175, 177–8, 181
Rowling, J.K.
    *Harry Potter* novels 168–74
        fantasy and reality in 169–70
        theme of good and evil in 170–1

St John's Gospel, opening lines 19–21
satire *see under* Swift, *Gulliver's Travels*
Sayers, Dorothy L. 115

214

# Index